The Pentateuch

The Continuum Biblical Studies Series

SERIES EDITOR: STEVE MOYISE

The Continuum Biblical Studies Series is aimed at those taking a course of biblical studies. Developed for the use of those embarking on theological and ministerial education, it is equally helpful in local church situations, and for lay people confused by apparently conflicting approaches to the Scriptures.

Students of biblical studies today will encounter a diversity of interpretive positions. Their teachers will – inevitably – lean towards some positions of preference to others. This series offers an integrated approach to the Bible which recognizes this diversity, but helps readers to understand it, and to work towards some kind of unity within it.

This is an ecumenical series, written by Roman Catholics and Protestants. The writers are all professionally engaged in the teaching of biblical studies in theological and ministerial education. The books are the product of that experience, and it is the intention of the editor, Dr Steve Moyise, that their contents should be tested on this exacting audience.

The Pentateuch
A Story of Beginnings

PAULA GOODER

CONTINUUM
London and New York

Continuum
The Tower Building, 11 York Road, London SE1 7NX
370 Lexington Avenue, New York, NY 10017-6503

First published 2000

British Library Cataloguing-in-Publication Data
A catalogue record for this book is available from the British Library.
ISBN 0-8264-5149-7

Typeset by BookEns Ltd, Royston Herts
Printed and bound in Great Britain by TJ International Ltd, Padstow, Cornwall

Contents

Acknowledgements

Thanks are due to many people who, in their different ways, have contributed to the writing of this book. I first began thinking about issues surrounding the interpretation of the Pentateuch through my teaching at Ripon College Cuddesdon and would like to extend my thanks to all those students who have helped me to think and rethink my ideas.

Thanks are also due to John Davies for his tireless efforts in the library of Ripon College Cuddesdon, tracking down references and seeking out new publications when I needed them. I am also grateful for the help of Catherine Grylls and my husband, Peter Babington, who read drafts of this book and offered helpful comments for its improvement.

I dedicate this book to my daughter, Susannah Joy, whose own beginnings took place while I wrote it.

1

Introduction

A story of beginnings

Beginnings are important. Throughout the course of history, people have wanted to know their origins. The answers to questions such as who our ancestors were, where they came from and what caused them to settle in one place and not another, allow us to understand a little about ourselves. History matters, not simply because it describes what happened in the past, but also because it helps us to understand the present. Our understanding of the world around can often be illuminated by knowledge of past events and relationships. History may also point forward to the future. An understanding of what caused various things to happen in the past can enable us to imagine what the future might hold. People whose historical foundations are firm often gain a strong sense of present and future identity. Beginnings are important not simply because they describe how things used to be but because they can also point to how things might be.

This is especially true of the accounts of beginnings found in the Bible. They not only describe how the world came to be but also point to the on-going relationship between God and humanity. The accounts were intended to be not so much informative as inspirational. They aimed to open a window on to how the world might be in relationship with the God who began the world and who continually intervenes in its history. The first five books of the Bible, often called the Pentateuch, provide an account of the beginnings of the people of God. On one level this statement is obvious. Genesis begins by describing creation: the beginning of the whole world. Yet, on reading further, it becomes clear that the whole of the Pentateuch is describing the beginnings of the people of God, starting with the creation and ending on the banks of the river Jordan, as the people who follow Moses prepare to enter the Promised Land. The theme of creation is present not only in the formation of the world but also in the formation of Israel as the people of God. As the narrative unfolds, the creation of Israel is revealed.

The purpose of the first five books of the Hebrew Bible is to trace the creation and development of the people who eventually became 'Israelites'. The story is told from various perspectives, all of which aim to portray the developing relationship between God and God's people. It begins by describing the creation of the whole world, but slowly narrows its perspective from humanity as a whole to the particular chosen people of God and their journey to the land that God promised to them. The story, as told in the Pentateuch, ends on a hill overlooking the Promised Land. The people of God are close to their promised destination but have not, as yet, reached it. The five books end with a beginning: the beginning of the life of the people of God in the land that God has given them.

Thus the Pentateuch is a story of beginnings. It traces beginnings from the dawn of the world to the dawn of 'Israel'. The five books – Genesis, Exodus, Leviticus, Numbers and Deuteronomy – act as a prologue to what follows, pointing the reader to many of the major themes that will appear throughout Israel's history. Yet the Pentateuch is not simply descriptive. Its purpose is not only to recount what happened but also to give readers down the centuries a glimpse into what the world might be. Just as a knowledge of our own historical ancestors can convey a sense of identity, so also a knowledge of the ancestors of faith can provide readers of the Bible with a sense of religious identity and possibility.

Genesis to Deuteronomy within biblical tradition

The stories that are told in these five books are some of the best known stories in the Bible. The accounts of creation and flood, Joseph and his coat of many colours, Moses and the crossing of the Red Sea have caught the imagination of many people and have, to this day, formed the inspiration behind a wide variety of paintings and pieces of music. Indeed, the musical *Joseph and his Technicolor Dream Coat* by Andrew Lloyd Webber and Tim Rice, inspired by the story of Joseph, has been one of the most popular musicals ever written. These narratives have passed into popular imagination and are used over and over again as a source of inspiration for contemporary stories, paintings, films and music.

This was as true for the biblical writers as it is for modern authors, artists and musicians. The stories of the Pentateuch inspired not only their original narrators but also many other subsequent biblical authors. The narratives of the Pentateuch are often referred to elsewhere in the

Hebrew Bible and their influence can be found in varying forms in many other biblical books. Certain themes found in the Pentateuch are picked up either explicitly or implicitly throughout the Hebrew Bible. Examples of this include creation (Ps 148:5), God's covenant with the Patriarchs (2 Kings 13:23), exodus (Jer 2:6) and the giving of the law to Moses on Sinai (Neh 9:13). It also seems at least possible that later biblical writers knew the actual Pentateuch itself, as well as the stories it contains. An example of this is the book of Nehemiah, which describes Ezra reading to the people from the 'book of the law of Moses' after they had returned from exile (Neh 8:1–3). The book of Nehemiah does not record the words that were read but it does record what the people did as a result of hearing the law read by Ezra. The reforms that the people undertook as a result of hearing the book's contents seem to be inspired by the commandments of both Leviticus and Deuteronomy. Consequently many, though not all, scholars regard the book of the law from which Ezra read as being a part of the Pentateuch.

In addition to this, certain verses from the Pentateuch are quoted again and again in different contexts. An example of this is Exodus 34:6: 'The Lord, the Lord, a God merciful and gracious, slow to anger, and abounding in steadfast love and faithfulness'. This verse became a standard description of God in later biblical books and is used in numerous other passages, though its source is never identified (see, for example, Neh 9:17; Ps 86:15; 103:8; 145:8; Joel 2:13 and Jon 4:2).

The writers of the New Testament also made extensive use of the Pentateuch in various ways. Like the Hebrew Bible, the books of the New Testament contain allusions to the Pentateuch's narratives. These include references to the themes of the Pentateuch, as well as direct quotations. Allusions to themes such as creation (Mark 13:18; Rom 1:19), Abraham (Gal 4:22) and the appearance of God to Moses in the burning bush (Luke 20:37) abound both in the gospels and the later epistles. Quotations are also common: see, for example, Mark 10:6–7

> But from the beginning of creation, 'God made them male and female.'
> 'For this reason a man shall leave his father and mother and be joined to his wife.'

Here Mark has combined two quotes, one from Genesis 1:27 and the other from 2:24.

The apostle Paul also made frequent citations from the Pentateuch to support his argument. One of the most striking examples of this can be found in Romans 4, which contains a quotation from Genesis 15:6: 'And he [Abraham] believed the Lord; and the Lord reckoned it to him as righteousness.' Another interesting phenomenon in the New Testament is extended reflection upon portions of the Pentateuch.

For example, many scholars regard the prologue to the Gospel of John (John 1:1–18) as a meditation upon, among other texts, Genesis 1. A less well known example of this is the Colossians hymn (Col 1:15–20), which C. F. Burney (1926) suggested was an extended reflection on the very first word of Genesis 1:1, *bereshit*, normally translated 'In the beginning'.

The regular use of the Pentateuch by later biblical writers demonstrates that the stories and text of the Pentateuch are important not just in their own right, but also because of the influence they had on subsequent biblical writers. The stories they told of God and God's people, the theology they portrayed, even the phrases they used, were picked up and used again by later biblical writers. This story of beginnings was as significant for its earliest readers as it is for modern readers of the text. Anyone hoping to understand the biblical narrative as a whole must first steep themselves in the language and traditions of its first five books.

Naming Genesis to Deuteronomy

The first five books of the Bible are referred to in various ways. Within the Hebrew Bible itself, they are often referred to collectively as 'the law', 'the book of Moses', 'the law of the Lord', or some combination of these (see, for example, Ezra 7:10; 10:3; Neh 8:3; 8:18; Dan 9:11; Mal 4:4), although it is often unclear whether these titles refer to the first five books as a collection or just to parts of them. In Jewish tradition and parts of the New Testament they are also referred to as law (see, for example, Matt 12:5; Mark 12:26; Luke 2:23–24; John 7:23; Gal 3:10). Indeed, Hebrew Bibles are divided into three sections with the Hebrew names of *Torah* (law), *Nebi'im* (prophets) and *Ketubim* (writings). The first letter of the name of each section gives the acronym *Tanak*, by which many Jews refer to the Hebrew scriptures.

An alternative title, often used by Christian scholars, is 'Pentateuch', a word derived from Greek and meaning a five-volume work. This title refers simply to the number of books contained within the collection. Its value is that it makes no judgement about the books' content. However, even this title presents problems. Various scholars regard this collection not as a five-volume work but as a six-volume work ('Hexateuch') or as a four-volume work ('Tetrateuch'). Although he was not the first to propose it, J. Wellhausen made the idea of a Hexateuch popular at the end of the nineteenth century in his now famous book, published in English under the title *Prolegomena to the History of Israel*. In addition to the five books, Genesis to Deuteronomy, the Hexateuch also included the book of Joshua. Reasons for this lie in the source-critical approach to the text, which we will consider in Chapter 2. The effect of this theory is to end the sweep of the narrative in the Promised Land itself, rather than on the brink of it as with the 'Pentateuch'. While this raises other interesting questions about the text, it detracts from the theme of beginnings and the creation of 'land', first for the world and then for Israel.

In contrast to Wellhausen, M. Noth proposed not a Hexateuch but a Tetrateuch. In his seminal work, published in English under the title of *The Deuteronomistic History* ([1943] 1981), he argued that the book of Deuteronomy did not form the conclusion to the books of Genesis to Numbers but instead acted as a prologue to what the Hebrew Bible terms the 'Former prophets' (Joshua to 2 Kings). Without its fifth book, the books of Genesis to Numbers become a Tetrateuch instead of a Pentateuch. Again, this proposal provided some significant insights into the initial books of the Hebrew Bible but lost the impact of ending the collection on the brink of entry into the Promised Land.

The theories that suggest that the initial books of the Hebrew Bible should be regarded either as a Hexateuch or as a Tetrateuch are significant in so far as they offer insights into the connection between the first five books of the Bible and those which follow. This allows us to view these books as a part of the whole biblical narrative, not just an isolated collection. The disadvantage of these theories, however, is that they detract from the narrative structure of the Pentateuch in its present form. This factor, alongside the existence of the tradition, within both Judaism and Christianity, of reading the first five books as one collection, suggests that the title 'Pentateuch' for the books Genesis to Deuteronomy is a helpful one.

Genesis to Deuteronomy within Jewish tradition

The Torah occupies a central position within Jewish beliefs and devotion. We have already noted its significance within the rest of the Hebrew Bible. This significance became even more pronounced in later Jewish tradition. *Pirke Avot* 1:1, a tractate in the Mishnah which was compiled around the end of the second century CE, records the belief that Moses received the Torah (not just the Ten Commandments) on Mount Sinai. It goes on to say that Torah was made up of two parts, 'written law' and 'oral law'. Both were passed down from generation to generation: the 'written law' in the form of the biblical Torah and the 'oral law' in the teachings of the Rabbis.

It has been a common misconception that legalism is a central element of a Jewish understanding of Torah. This is, in fact, far from the truth. Although Jewish devotion to the Torah recognizes its legal element, it encompasses much more than this. The medieval Jewish philosopher Maimonides maintained that the Torah was concerned with the welfare of both the body and the soul (*Guide of the Perplexed* 3:27). This belief illustrates that, within Judaism, the Torah holds the central place of devotion because it guides the whole of human existence. Various traditions grew up in Jewish thought about the Torah and its contents. One of these is that the Torah was pre-existent before the creation of the world, alongside wisdom. This tradition can be found both in the deutero-canonical book Ecclesiasticus (see, for example, 1:1–5; 34:8) and in later Jewish interpretation of the Torah (see, for example, *Genesis Rabbah* 1:4). Another tradition grew up around the account of creation in Genesis 1:1–2:3. The writings of the Mishnah indicate that certain portions of scripture became the subject of mystical speculation. This mystical speculation, known as Merkabah mysticism, was regarded as dangerous in some circles, especially to the uninitiated. Indeed, *Mishnah Hagigah* 2:1 forbids the exposition of the account of creation because of the danger which might befall an inexperienced person:

> The laws of forbidden sexual relations [Lev 18 and 20] may not be expounded by three persons, nor the account of creation [Gen 1:1–2:3] by two, nor the merkabah [Ezek 1] by one, unless he is a scholar and has understood on his own.

The tradition associating Genesis 1:1-2:3 with mystical speculation became known as *ma'aseh bereshit* or the workings of creation.

In addition to its importance for private study and devotion, the Torah has a central role within Jewish liturgy. Each year, it is read from beginning to end in the synagogue services. Each service contains a reading from the Torah and a reading from the Prophets. This coupling of the reading from the Prophets with the reading from the Torah is known as the *haftorah* or completion of the Torah. This practice existed from an early stage in the history of worship in the synagogue and references to it can be found in New Testament passages such as Luke 4:17 and Acts 13:15.

Genesis to Deuteronomy in Christian tradition

Within Christian tradition, the Pentateuch, as a collection, has been less central. Within Jewish tradition, the first section of the Hebrew scriptures – Torah – has precedence over the other two sections; within Christian tradition, all sections of the Hebrew Bible are regarded more or less equally. This diminished significance of the first five books may be attributed to numerous factors, most obviously the shift in attention to the New Testament texts and their portrayal of the life of Jesus and the development of the early church.

Another factor may be the edition of the Bible used. The Vulgate is the Latin text of the Bible, traditionally attributed to St Jerome, and it was the major version of the Bible used within the Western church until the time of the Reformation. Although the Vulgate was based on both Greek and Hebrew texts, it followed the order of the Septuagint rather than that of the Hebrew texts (an order still maintained in modern Christian translations of the Bible). One of the effects of this was the abandonment of the traditional tri-partite ordering of the books into Torah, Prophets and Writings. Although Genesis to Deuteronomy remained in the same order at the beginning of the Bible, they were no longer gathered into a single collection as in the Hebrew texts. Thus, although Genesis to Deuteronomy remained important within Christianity as books in their own right, the five books viewed together, as a collection, became less significant.

Concluding remarks

The theme of 'beginnings' is a helpful way to view the books of Genesis to Deuteronomy. Not only do they contain stories that point to the beginnings of early Israel; they also provide a foundation for the biblical narrative as a whole. As well as setting the scene for the unfolding of the 'history of Israel', they provide a thematic and textual basis for the works of subsequent biblical writers. The themes and text of the Pentateuch feature regularly throughout both the Hebrew Bible and the Christian New Testament. Consequently, the Pentateuch is a narrative of 'beginnings' in more than one sense. It both describes the foundations of the world and Israel and also provides foundations for the rest of the biblical narrative. In the light of this, it seems fitting that much of biblical scholarship also finds its 'beginnings' in the Pentateuch. Many techniques used by scholars to understand biblical texts originated in Pentateuchal scholarship and approaches to the Pentateuch provided the foundations for many scholarly interpretations of the text.

The rest of this book will be concerned with exploring this theme further. Chapter 2, 'Beginning to read the Pentateuch' will consider the different ways in which scholars have begun to study the Pentateuch. Chapters 3 to 7 will examine the content, themes and scholarship of smaller sections of the Pentateuch, looking in turn at primeval history (Chapter 3); the patriarchal narratives (Chapter 4); the exodus (Chapter 5); the law codes (Chapter 6); and the wilderness wanderings (Chapter 7). Chapter 8 will draw together the ideas raised by the earlier chapters in some concluding remarks. Throughout the book, the text of the Pentateuch will be considered with the help of many different readings. Some will be drawn from the historical-critical school which seeks to establish the historical events that lie behind the narrative; others will be drawn from readings which focus either on the text itself or the experience of different readers of the text. All will be chosen with the aim of illuminating, as far as possible, the content of the Pentateuch but also of illustrating how the theme of 'beginnings' helps us to understand it better.

2

Beginning to read the Pentateuch

Introduction

The writings of the Pentateuch have played a significant role in Hebrew Bible scholarship. Although their role, as a collection, was less pronounced within Christian tradition than within Jewish tradition, they have been central to a large number of scholarly debates. Many leading Hebrew Bible scholars have written influential works on these first five books of the Bible. Indeed, the role of the Pentateuch as a story of beginnings is as true within scholarship as it is within the narrative itself. Studies of the Pentateuch have often been at the cutting edge of scholarly trends in biblical studies. Consequently, it is valuable to understand the origins and aims of such approaches to the text of the Pentateuch. This chapter will concentrate on approaches that have been applied to the Pentateuch as a whole. Approaches which consider individual narratives within books of the Pentateuch will feature in subsequent chapters.

As in much biblical scholarship, the issue which has most exercised scholars until recently is that of the origins of the text. Scholars have been most concerned with questions about who wrote it, where it came from and when its traditions originated. More recently, however, other concerns have been raised, such as how the text functions as a piece of literature and what central themes can be seen running throughout the collection. Finding answers to questions such as these has considerably enhanced our understanding of the text.

Who wrote the Pentateuch?

Problems in the text

Thus far, our consideration of the Pentateuch has assumed that the books, Genesis to Deuteronomy, form one continuous narrative from the creation of the world to the arrival of the people who fled from Egypt at the borders of the Promised Land. While the Pentateuch does have an overarching structure, such a description oversimplifies the text we have before us. Even the most superficial reading indicates that the Pentateuch contains a variety of literary styles: flowing narratives are placed next to genealogical lists; complex law codes appear alongside elaborate visions of God. The narrative of the Pentateuch does not flow seamlessly from beginning to end; rather, the story develops in leaps and bounds, told using a variety of different genres. A closer examination reveals certain inconsistencies in the text and some stories appear to be told two or three times, in different ways. The table below gives some examples of this.

Table 1: Some examples of doublets and triplets in the Pentateuch

1. Creation of humanity (Gen 1:26)	Creation of Adam (Gen 2:7)	
2. Flood waters continue for 40 days (Gen 7:17)	Flood waters continue for 150 days (Gen 7:24)	
3. Abraham passes off Sarah as his sister (Gen 12:10–20)	Abraham passes off Sarah as his sister (Gen 20:1–18)	Isaac passes off Rebekah as his sister (Gen 26:1–11)
4. Joseph's brothers agree to sell him to some Ishmaelites (Gen 37:28)	Joseph's brothers sell him to some Midianites (Gen 37:27)	
5. Moses goes up the mountain at the command of the Lord (Exod 24:1–2)	Moses goes up the mountain at the command of the Lord (Exod 24:9–11)	Moses goes up the mountain at the command of the Lord (Exod 24:15–18)
6. Joshua is appointed as leader of the people (Num 27:18–23)	Joshua is appointed as leader of the people (Deut 31:23)	

Mosaic authorship of the Pentateuch

The presence of different writing styles and various inconsistencies within the Pentateuch has raised questions about whether it was written by a single hand. This, in its turn, cast doubt on the traditional belief that Moses was its author. The tradition of the Mosaic authorship of the Pentateuch arose from the statement in Deuteronomy 31:9 that

'Moses wrote down this law, and gave it to the priests, the sons of Levi, who carried the ark of the covenant of the Lord, and to all the elders of Israel'. This law was understood to be the whole of the Pentateuch, not just the law spoken by Moses to the people in Deuteronomy. Consequently, by the time of Ezra, these five books were known as 'the book of Moses'. This became the traditional view on the authorship of the Pentateuch. It can be found in numerous Jewish and Christian texts (see, for example, Ecclus 24:23; Flavius Josephus, *The Antiquities of the Jews* 4:326; the Mishnah *Pirke Avot* 1.1; and various New Testament texts such as Mark 12:26).

The problem with this tradition is not just the variety of writing styles. Other factors also raise questions about the likelihood of Mosaic authorship. One difficulty is that Moses' death is reported in the Pentateuch itself, though this is not an insurmountable problem because it is recorded at the very end of the book of Deuteronomy (Deut 34:5). Rather more problematic is the list of Edomite kings in Genesis 36:31–39. As these kings lived a long time after the death of Moses, it seems unlikely that he could have written the list. Its presence within the Pentateuch questions the authenticity of the tradition that attributes the collection to Moses. Evidence such as this casts doubt on whether Moses could have written these five books. Indeed, the seventeenth-century philosopher Benedictus de Spinoza concluded that 'it is ... clearer than the sun at noonday that the Pentateuch was not written by Moses but by someone who lived long after Moses' (cited in Blenkinsopp, 1992, p. 2). If Spinoza's observation is correct and Moses was not the sole author of the Pentateuch, then others must have been involved in writing it. Attempts to identify who the author or authors might have been have played an important part in scholarly examination of these five books.

Source criticism

Julius Wellhausen and the Documentary Hypothesis

We have already noted that the text of the Pentateuch contains various inconsistencies and repetitions, which interrupt the smooth flow of the narrative. A closer examination of these inconsistencies indicates that, in many places where stories are repeated, the narrative style and the name used for God are different. In addition, scholars have noted that it is often possible to link the use of certain terminology with a certain literary style. For example, texts that use the divine name YHWH (translated in English Bibles as 'the Lord') for God also regularly have a flowing literary style; some texts which use the term '*elohim* (translated in English Bibles as 'God') have a more disjointed, list-like style.

While there is a certain level of inconsistency between accounts, it is possible to identify strands within the Pentateuch, which use the same style and terminology. This suggests that these are not random inconsistencies in the text, but follow certain patterns. This, in its turn, raises the possibility that the text of the Pentateuch reached its present form as the result of the conflation of more than one original source, gathered together by an editor or redactor. The attempt to identify the different sources that lie behind the biblical text is known as 'source criticism'; the theory that identifies four separate sources behind the Pentateuch, in particular, is termed the 'Documentary Hypothesis'.

The notion that a number of sources lay behind the final text of the Pentateuch was raised as early as the seventeenth century. During the following two centuries, scholars debated the number and dating of these possible sources. In 1883, J. Wellhausen set out the 'Documentary Hypothesis' in its classic formulation in his now famous *Prolegomena to the History of Israel* (first translated into English in 1885). The significance of Wellhausen's theory lay not in his enumeration of four sources, since that had been done before, but in the order he proposed for their composition. This proposal rapidly became accepted in scholarly circles.

The four sources of the Pentateuch proposed by source critics are the Yahwist Source (abbreviated as 'J' from the German 'Jahvist'), the Elohist Source ('E'), the Deuteronomic Source ('D') and the Priestly Source ('P'). Source critics identify each source according to certain characteristics laid out in Table 2 opposite. The principle which lies behind the division of the text into these sources is that the consistent use of terminology and literary style identifies and differentiates the writings of one source from the others. The application of these basic characteristics to the text allows the source critic to identify the source in which each unit of text originated. Indeed, tables which divide the Pentateuch verse by verse into the four sources have been produced (see particularly the appendix to Noth, [1948] 1972, and Campbell and O'Brien, 1993).

Wellhausen used this technique to identify the different sources of the Pentateuch. Once he had done this, he examined the major characteristics of the sources in an attempt to date them. He maintained that 'J' and 'E' were written first and joined together by an editor after their composition. Interestingly, Wellhausen did not always differentiate between these two sources and often referred to them as 'JE'. Likewise, he did not attempt to date either source more precisely than 'in the monarchical period' (the dates given in Table 2

below originate from the work of subsequent scholarship). He placed
'D' next, on the grounds that 'D' seemed to know 'JE' but not 'P', and
maintained that 'P' was the last to be written. Wellhausen used source
critical principles on the book of Joshua as well as on Genesis to
Deuteronomy. As a result he identified the presence of a 'Hexateuch'
(six books), not just a 'Pentateuch' (five books).

One motivation behind Wellhausen's dating of the different sources
was his belief that Israel's religious history developed over a period of
time and that it is possible to trace this development in the different
sources of the Pentateuch. Wellhausen believed that religions began as
a spontaneous expression arising from the events of everyday life. Then,
as it developed, it became more institutional and eventually lost all
spontaneity. Consequently, he regarded 'JE' as the earliest sources,
containing evidence of spontaneous worship, followed by 'D' with its
interest in centralising the worship of Israel and, last of all, 'P' and its
insistence on correct legal and ritual observance.

Table 2: The major characteristics of the sources of the Documentary Hypothesis

Source	Yahwist Source ('J')	Elohist Source ('E')	Deuteronomic Source ('D')	Priestly Source ('P')
Name for God	Yahweh	God ('elohim or 'el)	Yahweh	God ('elohim or 'el)
Name for Sinai/Horeb	Sinai	Horeb	Horeb	Sinai
Concentration on particular part of Israel	Judah	Northern Israel (Ephraim)	Judah	Whole of Israel
Major characteristics	Primeval history	No primeval history	No primeval history	Primeval history
	Flowing narrative style with concentration on lives of Patriarchs	Epic style

Strong moral tone | No narrative: collection of exhortatory and legal material

Long speeches

Stress on Jerusalem | Interest in dates and order

Genealogies

Interest in cultic ritual and law |
| | Etymology of words often given | | | |

Table 2: continued

Source	Yahwist Source ('J')	Elohist Source ('E')	Deuteronomic Source ('D')	Priestly Source ('P')
Characteristics of God	God described in human terms	God often speaks in dreams	God's covenant with Israel	God viewed as transcendent
		Frequent references to fear of God		
Possible date of composition	c. 950–850 BCE	c. 850–750 BCE	622 BCE onwards but before 'P'	Late exilic/ early post exilic, before Ezra

Hebrew Bible scholars rapidly accepted this version of a 'Documentary Hypothesis', with JEDP written in that order. Indeed, this understanding of the history of the composition of the Pentateuch has been one of the most influential theories in Hebrew Bible scholarship in the twentieth century and has given rise to numerous further theories aimed at uncovering the Pentateuch's origins.

The extent of the impact of the Documentary Hypothesis is evident in the difficulties that face anyone who attempts to trace its development. This theory is so influential that a whole host of different theories have grown out of it. Indeed, it is somewhat ironic that the current crisis which surrounds the hypothesis is as much due to the theories that set out to support it as to those that set out to criticize it. The wealth of proposals and counter-proposals that developed out of the original theory are now so complex that the hypothesis struggles to survive. The various studies which grew out of the theory attempted to discover different things about the process of the composition of the Pentateuch. Some tried to discover more about the stories that make up the Pentateuch before they were written down; others turned their attention in more detail to the sources themselves and attempted to define them more precisely than the early source critics had. E.W. Nicholson (1998) has recently produced a thorough, up-to-date survey of scholarly treatments of the Pentateuch, which examines the field in detail; a shorter treatment can be found in J. Van Seters (1999, pp. 30–86).

Form criticism and oral tradition

H. Gunkel ([1901] 1964), though never questioning the validity of the Documentary Hypothesis, was more interested in the oral tradition that lay behind the sources than in the sources themselves. He imagined the early Israelites telling and retelling the stories of their earliest history many times before they came to be written down. Consequently, Gunkel hoped to be able to rediscover something about these stories before they were written down. Most importantly, he maintained that these stories were remembered and told for a specific reason and were therefore to be regarded as 'aetiologies' or legends told to explain why things are as they are. The method that Gunkel developed to enable him to achieve his goal is known as 'form criticism' because of his insistence that the form of a story can tell us a lot about its history. He applied his interest in form criticism to the Psalter as well as to Genesis and this theory greatly influenced subsequent study of the Psalms.

Gunkel's theories, in their turn, influenced two other great Hebrew Bible scholars: G. von Rad ([1938] 1966) and M. Noth ([1948] 1972). Both of them were convinced of the importance of a 'pre-literary' stage in the composition of the Pentateuch and sought to reconstruct it. Like Gunkel they believed that the stories were remembered for specific reasons, though unlike him they identified the worship of ancient Israel as the reason for their retelling. Thus they maintained that the stories of the Pentateuch were preserved because of their use in the 'cultic life' or worship of Israel.

More complex considerations of the Documentary Hypothesis

One important task for scholars seeking to support the Documentary Hypothesis was to understand more about each individual source and its role in the composition of the Pentateuch as a whole. This attempt has played an important part in recent studies on the Pentateuch. As these studies have tended to concentrate more on one source than on all of them, we shall examine the major proposals affecting each source in turn.

The Yahwist Source

The Yahwist Source has been the subject of considerable further discussion. Suggested alterations to the original theory have centred on three major areas: the identification of different strands within 'J'; the consideration of 'J' as a creative theologian; and the redating of 'J' to a much later period. Many scholars have suggested that the basic 'J' source is made up of more than one strand within the source, normally indicated by a number or letter in superscript or subscript (for example, J^1 or J_b). Others maintain the presence of an earlier strand out of which the 'J' and 'E' sources emerged (Noth calls this 'G' from the German *Grundlage*, meaning foundation). A. de Pury reviews theories relating to 'J' in his article 'Yahwist 'J' Source' in *The Anchor Bible Dictionary* (1992, pp. 1013–20).

Von Rad's theory moved in the opposite direction. Despite his interest in the pre-literary background to the Pentateuch, von Rad was convinced that the 'Yahwist' was a creative theologian who stamped his own personality on his writing. Indeed, von Rad believed that the 'Yahwist' was one of the greatest theologians ever to write:

> As regards the creative genius of the Yahwist's narrative there is only admiration. Someone has justly called the artistic mastery in this narrative one of the greatest accomplishments of all times in the history of thought. (von Rad, [1956] 1972, p. 25)

Various scholars, including Noth ([1948] 1972), also regard 'J' as a theologian, though few join von Rad in viewing the 'Yahwist' as a single person. A much more radical response to the Documentary Hypothesis has been to redate 'J' (and indeed the whole of the Pentateuch) to the exilic period. J. Van Seters has argued extensively that 'J' was written as a prologue to the history of Israel to be found in the books of Joshua to 2 Kings and therefore should be dated much later than Wellhausen first proposed. He further proposed that it was 'J' and not 'P' that provided the unifying basis for the Pentateuch as a whole. Instead he regards 'P' as 'composed from the start as a supplementation to the earlier work' (1999, p. 211). This position is argued in detail in his 1983 book on historiography and a shorter summary of his views can be found in his 1999 commentary on the Pentateuch, pp. 112–59.

The Elohist Source

'E' is the most commonly questioned source of the Documentary Hypothesis. The reason for this is the difficulty in differentiating it from 'J', and even Wellhausen himself often referred to 'JE' as a source. We have seen already that scholars such as Noth explain this as due to their basis in a common source. Others go so far as to suggest that the source 'E' should be abandoned altogether (see the discussion in Blenkinsopp, 1992, p. 14).

The Deuteronomic Source

From the beginning, 'D' has always had a slightly unusual position in the Documentary Hypothesis. While the other sources are seen as being spread relatively evenly throughout the first four books of the

Pentateuch, the vast majority of 'D' is thought to be contained in the book of Deuteronomy. A crucial question for source critics is how much of 'D' can be found in Genesis to Numbers (the Tetrateuch). If the answer is none, the Deuteronomic Source has little part to play in the Documentary Hypothesis as a whole. In recent years scholars such as J. Blenkinsopp have argued for 'a more extensive D editing of the history from Abraham to Moses than the classical Documentary Hypothesis contemplated' (Blenkinsopp, 1992, p. 236). The effect of this theory is to move 'D' into a more central position within the Documentary Hypothesis.

The Priestly Source

Advances in studies on the Priestly Source mirror the three major areas of development identified for the Yahwist Source. Interest has focused around locating more than one strand in the source, understanding the creative impulse of the writer or school of writers and attempting to re-date the source. Wellhausen, himself, noted that there was a distinction between the narrative material of the Priestly Source and the legal material. Many subsequent scholars have supported this position, though there is not entire agreement as to what should count as narrative and what as legal material. Noth's abbreviation of P^g to refer to narrative material and P^s to refer to legal material is the most common, though not the only, way of referring to possible different strands within the source.

In addition, many regard the Priestly Source as comprising a number of pre-existing sources, two of the best known being the 'book of generations' (or *toledot*, from the Hebrew word for generations) and 'the Holiness Code'. The theory about the 'book of generations' arises from the fact that the Pentateuch is punctuated in various places with long lists of genealogies. These begin with the Hebrew phrase *sepher toledot*, literally the 'book of generations' (though translated in the NRSV as 'the list of the descendants' – see, for example, Gen 5:1). It is at least possible that these genealogies formed an original source, later incorporated into the Priestly Source. The 'Holiness Code', sometimes called 'H', can be found in Leviticus 17–26. It is a collection of laws stressing the importance for Israel of being holy. Its language and theology suggest that it is separate from the rest of the book of Leviticus. Traditional theories about its origin maintain that it pre-dates the Priestly Source, though I. Knohl (1987) maintains that it emerged from a holiness school who were writing after 'P' to correct it.

This use of pre-existing sources raises questions about the Priestly Source's creative role in the formation of the Pentateuch. Since Wellhausen, most scholars have regarded 'P' as the last source to be written and often as responsible for redacting the Pentateuch into its current form. F. M. Cross (1973) went even further and suggested that 'P' was much more important as a redactor than as a source. He argues that the 'P' material present in the Pentateuch is so scanty that at best it can only be regarded as the 'précis of P' (p. 294), not the whole narrative. 'P' was responsible for structuring the Pentateuch into its current form but contains little material from an original Priestly Source. In contrast to this minimal view of the Priestly Source, other scholars have a higher view of the source. N. Lohfink (1994) believes that it is possible to identify a priestly historical narrative and gives a detailed breakdown of the texts he includes within it (Lohfink, 1994, p. 145, n. 29).

A. Hurwitz (1982) is more concerned with the dating of the source. He and others have argued in favour of a pre-exilic date for the Priestly Source on linguistic and theological grounds. He compared the language of the Priestly Source with that of Ezekiel and post-exilic texts and maintained that the language of the Priestly Writer was earlier. One of the motivations behind this argument is a fundamental opposition to Wellhausen's theory of the development of the religion of Israel outlined above. Wellhausen's dislike of Judaism as a religious system is well known. His theory that Judaism developed from spontaneous worship to an institutionalised religion dominated by priests arises from this dislike. This has led various scholars, particularly those of a Jewish background, to question the basis of his judgement on the dating of the sources which lie behind the Pentateuch.

Alternative approaches to the Pentateuch

For a long time, a broad consensus existed among scholars about the nature and dating of the Pentateuch's sources. The brief survey given above demonstrates that this consensus no longer exists. Various factors have led people to question the hypothesis. Perhaps one of the most important problems is the increasing lack of certainty about the Pentateuch's origins. For many years, the origins of the Pentateuch were regarded as fixed. 'J' and 'E' wrote first, followed by 'D' and ending with 'P', who may also have redacted the Pentateuch into the form which we now possess. The veracity of this hypothesis is no longer as accepted as it used to be. There are an increasing variety of opinions on the number of strands in each source. Many scholars now uphold the likelihood of numerous traditions behind the written sources. The dating of each source is less certain and some scholars have even questioned the existence of four sources.

This lack of certainty about the reliability of the four-source hypothesis has raised questions about the primacy of its position as a tool by which scholars interpret the Pentateuch. This is exacerbated by the general movement in biblical studies away from merely historical-critical approaches to other more literary and theological considerations (described in more detail in S. Moyise, 1998). Some theories, like the Documentary Hypothesis, are interested in discovering the origins of the Pentateuch; others concentrate their attention on the themes or theology of the text; while others still are interested in different ways of interpreting the text. In many cases, attention has moved away from attempts to interpret the whole of Pentateuch to an interest in the interpretation of individual passages. We will consider these studies below as we look in more detail at each book of the Pentateuch. Others, however, still attempt to look at the Pentateuch as a whole and it is to these studies that we now turn.

Alternative attempts to identify the origins of the Pentateuch

Despite the popularity of the Documentary Hypothesis, other proposals to explain the origins of the Pentateuch have existed for many years. One of the most significant is that of R. Rendtorff (1990). Rendtorff was influenced by the scholarship of von Rad and Noth but, unlike them, considered that their theories concerning oral tradition placed the Documentary Hypothesis in question. He turned his attention to the units of tradition such as primeval history, patriarchal narratives, the exodus, the giving of the law at Sinai and the wandering in the wilderness. He maintained that these units of tradition did not contain continuous strands but were independent units that had developed separately and been joined together by a later redactor. This theory refutes the basis of the Documentary Hypothesis that the Pentateuch contains continuous sources that stretch from beginning to end, in favour of numerous smaller units originally unrelated to each other.

Alternative, though similar, approaches can be found in the work of N. Whybray and U. Cassuto. Whybray (1987) argues strongly against the prevailing tendency within scholarship to view the Pentateuch as having reached its final form over a long period of time as the result of repeated redaction. Instead, he viewed it as the product of one particular author who used artistic flair to combine various sources into the shape of the present Pentateuch. The most radical notion of his theory is that the sources used by this dynamic author were not necessarily very old. U. Cassuto argued along similar lines that the author of the Pentateuch used prose legends and epic poems to form the Pentateuch. He argued that the different names for God used in the Pentateuch were not due to a dependence on different sources, but reflected different aspects of God's persona. As much of Cassuto's work on the Pentateuch was written in either Italian or Hebrew, his theories have not been easily accessible to English-speaking students. They have, however, recently been summarized by A. Rofé (1999, pp. 104–11), whose treatment of Cassuto's work provides a helpful introduction to his major proposals.

In his book *Introduction to the Composition of the Pentateuch* (1999), Rofé presents his own solution to the question of the Pentateuch's origins. He believes that the earliest origins of the Pentateuch lie in oral legend and epic poem, which were joined together into a 'single chain of history'. The final form of the Pentateuch was achieved by the joining together of three great schools: 'D' (the Deuteronomic School) and two schools from the priestly tradition, 'H' (the Holiness Code) and 'P' (the Priestly School). 'D', 'H' and 'P' in Rofé's proposal all correspond roughly to the 'D', 'H' and 'P' strands identified elsewhere. The major difference is that rather than attributing material to a 'JE' strand, Rofé maintains that 'P' took over the 'single chain of history' formed from legends and epic poems and crafted it into an overall narrative. Rofé can thus be seen to stand somewhere between traditional source critical theory and the more modern views of Rendtorff, Whybray and Cassuto.

Alternative attempts to understand the theology of the Pentateuch

Another trend in Hebrew Bible studies is to abandon the attempt to understand the origins of the Pentateuch in favour of understanding it in its present form. This moves the attention away from the historical events behind the text to the theology within it. It has taken a variety of forms but is well illustrated by the work of two influential scholars N. Lohfink and D. J. A. Clines. Lohfink identifies a number of major themes in the Priestly and Deuteronomic Sources, whereas Clines locates an overarching theme for the whole of the Pentateuch.

Lohfink (1994) accepts the basic premise of sources that lie behind the Pentateuch and from here examines some of the major themes that he identifies within 'P' and 'D'. This takes the form of looking in detail at certain individual passages but also of examining certain themes within the sources. An interesting example is his article, 'The Priestly Narrative and History', which, as its title suggests, explores the understanding of history to be found in the writings of the Priestly Writer. Lohfink maintains that the Priestly narrative was written with a specific audience and purpose in mind. He argues that it was written for the people in exile to encourage them and give them hope for the future. Lohfink regards the priestly stories as 'paradigmatic', that is they present an example of how Israel could be. Within the narrative, the world falls 'repeatedly from its perfect form into the imperfection of becoming' (p. 172). This challenges the readers in exile to re-enter the process and to return to the pattern of things intended by God.

A similar, though more radical, view is that of D. J. A. Clines (1997). Rather than examining the theme of one source within the Pentateuch, Clines chooses to examine the theme of the 'final form' of the Pentateuch, i.e. what we have now. The motivation behind this is a recognition of the importance of the Pentateuch as a collection within both the Jewish and Christian traditions. Clines identifies the theme of the Pentateuch as 'the partial fulfilment – which implies also the partial non-fulfilment – of the promise to or blessing of the patriarchs' (p. 30). He maintains that this promise has three elements: posterity, divine–human relationship and land. These, he maintains, are interdependent: a promise from YHWH must involve a divine–human relationship, which gains value by being for posterity and including land. He identifies that what he regards as the three major sections of the Pentateuch, Genesis 12–50, Exodus and Leviticus, and Numbers and Deuteronomy, each contain one element of this triple promise. Genesis 12–50 is concerned with posterity through the promise to Abraham; Exodus and Leviticus, focus on the divine–human relationship and Numbers and Deuteronomy explore the concept of land.

The obvious problem with Clines' theory, which he recognizes, is that it leaves little space for Genesis 1–11, as the narrative of these chapters pre-dates the patriarchal promise. Clines views these chapters as containing what he calls a 'prefatory theme' (pp. 66–86). By this, he means that Genesis 1–11 sets the scene for the rest of the Pentateuchal narrative. He proposes that Genesis 1–11 sets forth the message that, despite their propensity for destroying God's good creation, God always delivers humanity from the consequences of their sins. This sets the scene for God's promise to Abraham in Genesis 12.

In addition to these, two other recent studies present similar aims. T. D. Alexander (1995), like Lohfink, concentrated his attention on a number of themes that he found within the Pentateuch; unlike Lohfink, however, he based his findings on a narrative reading of the text, not on source criticism. His understanding of the Pentateuch is that it consists of numerous diverse themes brought together to form the unifying theme of God's relationship with the descendants of Abraham, Isaac and Jacob. T. E. Fretheim likewise chose to examine the Pentateuch in its present form but, like Clines, opted to identify an overarching theme which he defined as an intention within the text to 'shape the life and faith of its readers' (Fretheim, 1996, p. 62).

The value of approaches such as these is that they examine the content of the text – not simply the literary style and form, as was true of many source critics. Their work presents a refreshing contrast to the thorough but sometimes dry studies of source criticism. However, these proposals are all open to the criticism of subjectivity: the identification of the major themes of either one source or the whole Pentateuch could be seen to be 'in the eye of the beholder'. The factors that lead someone to identify a theme or themes as the central message of a book or collection of books can often be open to individual interpretation. Yet, in the current climate of biblical studies, where the value of a multiplicity of readings is recognized, such partiality is not considered unreasonable. Indeed, Clines, in the 1997 'Afterword' to his original 1978 book, recognizes this very point. Whereas he formerly considered the theme that he identified to be the meaning intended by the author, he would now regard it simply as the meaning that he himself encountered in the text and not necessarily what was originally intended (Clines, 1997, p. 133).

Alternative attempts to interpret the Pentateuch

This general shift in biblical studies means that subjectivity is no longer condemned. When source criticism was at its height, scholarly interest in the biblical texts was restricted to 'objective' historical concerns, that is, where the texts came from and how they reached their present form. The climate which produced the more complex and varied solutions to the problems of the authorship of the Pentateuch also produced an increased hesitancy about the assurance of their results. This lack of certainty allowed more and more solutions to be entertained, many of which seemed to be valuable. Since not all could be 'objectively true', readings which betrayed the interests and concerns of their authors became more acceptable. This encouraged the production of self-consciously subjective studies, that is, those which drew on the concerns of the person writing as much as on the text itself.

Liberationist and feminist readings are, perhaps, the best-known interpretations of this type. Both begin with the experience of oppression (in some form) by the readers of the text and use this as a tool to gain new insight into the message of the text in the modern context. A. Laffey (1998) has recently produced such a study on the Pentateuch. She calls her approach a 'liberation-critical reading' and draws inspiration from both feminist and liberationist readings of the text. The aim of the book is to draw out the theme of the 'interdependence of all the individual characters and types of characters portrayed in the Pentateuch' (p. 5).

Her goal is a positive one. Unlike many modern feminist readings of the Bible, which focus on the way in which the Bible has been used to silence women, Laffey regards the Bible as a liberating text. She aims to draw out the importance of reciprocity between all the characters of the pentateuchal narrative and thereby to affirm its importance in the mind of the modern reader. Through an examination of a selection of the most important texts within the Pentateuch, she demonstrates that this life-giving theme of reciprocity can be seen as a strand of central importance which runs throughout the first five books.

On the whole, few alternative attempts to interpret the Pentateuch direct their attention to the whole collection, Genesis to Deuteronomy. This is due to a general dissatisfaction with those theories which attempt to provide 'macro' solutions to the text. While a solution works well for one text, it rarely provides the answer for every text under consideration. Much more common among modern interpretations are 'micro' considerations, which look at the issues thrown up by one particular text but which do not attempt to extrapolate these to respond to the Pentateuch as a whole. These 'micro' solutions will be considered in more detail in the following chapters.

Concluding remarks

Pentateuchal scholarship is a vast and often impenetrable field. So many theories abound that it is hard for the student beginning a study of the Pentateuch to find a way in. The number of studies responding to the Documentary Hypothesis has exacerbated this problem in recent years. Responses range from a simplification of the original theory to an increasing complication of it; from basic support of the theory to outright rejection of it; from proposing a similar method to beginning again with an entirely new method of approach. The vast array of possible responses to the text only serve to demonstrate the Pentateuch's continuing importance within biblical studies as a whole.

3

In the beginning ...

Genesis 1–11: The world begins

The scene for our story of beginnings is set at the dawn of time. The author paints a picture of a watery chaos without form and entirely empty. A wind disturbs the waters and God begins to create. The first two chapters are taken up with a description of the process of creation. In chapter 3, the human beings created by God act and speak in their own right. Here begins one of the most important themes of Genesis 1–11, if not of the Pentateuch as a whole. Genesis 1–11 narrates a world finely balanced between good and evil. The cycle of good followed by imperfection followed by punishment, is one which rolls repeatedly throughout Genesis 1–11 and on into the rest of the narrative of the Pentateuch. Alongside this is a narrowing down of God's promises from humanity as a whole (in the persons of Adam and Eve), to righteous humanity (in the person of Noah). From there the reduction continues first to Abraham, the father of many nations and then to the nation of Israel alone.

The imperfection begins in Genesis 3 as Adam and Eve break the bounds placed upon them by God which prevents their eating from one of the trees in the garden. Their punishment is banishment from the garden and increased toil in the life God has given them. This pattern continues in Genesis 4 with the sin of their son Cain. In this account, Cain breaks the bounds placed on him by God, not this time as regards an inanimate tree, but as regards his own brother. His punishment is constant banishment: he must wander from place to place. Chapter 5 moves the narrative on through a number of generations to the time of Noah.

In Genesis 6:1–4 the pattern continues. This time, the 'sons of God' break the boundaries laid down by God and cross the boundary between heaven and earth to take mortals as their wives. Punishment is not declared but the flood immediately follows, and stands as a punishment against all humanity. Again, the punishment includes the theme of banishment: all animate creation is banished from the world made by God. The exception is Noah, his family and representative animals of all types who remain as recipients of God's promises. In Genesis 9:20–29 a new element to the pattern emerges: Ham sins against his father by looking upon his nakedness. Therefore he is condemned, not by God, but by his father. The narrative of Genesis 1–11 concludes with a final story of boundary breaking and banishment sandwiched between two genealogies. Here the boundaries between heaven and earth are threatened not by heavenly beings, as in chapter 6, but by human beings. The tower of Babel is built as an attempt to invade the heavenly realms. The punishment declared is banishment from one another: God prevents communication between peoples and scatters them across the world.

The pattern of Genesis 1–11, therefore, is of increasing violation of boundaries and the consequent increasing alienation of human beings. Certain boundaries are laid down to maintain the goodness of the creative order established by God. Attempts to cross these boundaries lead not to greater unity but to a greater separation. The boundary crossing begins with the crossing of the bounds laid down as regards the fruit of a tree and ends with an attempt to cross the bounds laid down between heaven and earth. Alienation begins with banishment from one ideal place and ends with the banishment of humans one from another. Nevertheless, the picture is not entirely dismal. God maintains a relationship with humanity throughout this cycle. As the alienation increases, so the relationship between God and humanity becomes more specific until God's own people are formed.

The existence of patterns in the narrative of Genesis 1–11 has long been recognized. D. J. A. Clines (1997) has pointed out that there is a significant pattern beyond that of sin and punishment. He identifies four elements in the pattern: sin, divine speech, mitigation and then punishment (pp. 66–70). Thus, he notes that between the sin and the punishment lies divine interaction with the sinner and a lessening of the intended punishment. Even in the midst of condemnation, God maintains a relationship with humanity.

The title and genre of Genesis 1–11

In the introduction, I referred to Genesis 1–11 as 'primeval history'. 'Primeval' (see, for example, von Rad, [1956] 1972, pp. 45–163) or 'primal' (see, for example, Westermann, 1988, pp. 1–4) history is the phrase often used by scholars to refer to the events described in Genesis 1–11 and is the term used generally by ancient historians to refer to a time that precedes recorded history. Accounts of primeval history exist in many cultures and are often concerned with the origins of the world.

Scholars regularly refer to the accounts contained within these 'primeval histories' as myths. This terminology can be difficult for those beginning study of the Pentateuch, not least because in modern parlance myth is used increasingly to mean something that is untrue. For some, the word myth evokes a fairytale: a story which is largely fictitious and not based upon fact. For others it is equated with 'urban myths', stories said to have happened to the 'friend of a friend' but never actually verified. When the biblical stories are referred to as 'myth', this is not what we mean. However, precisely what is meant by the term differs from scholar to scholar. There is immense difficulty in finding a definition of myth that encompasses both the biblical stories and the stories found in other literature. The problems that surround the modern use of the term myth are by no means new. Scholars of the late nineteenth and early twentieth century were also very hesitant about the use of the term. At this time, the Brothers Grimm, who defined myth as a tale about the gods, heavily influenced the definition of the word. This definition precluded the examination of the biblical narrative for 'myths', since the monotheistic framework of the Bible militated against its stories being regarded as tales about the gods.

Although modern scholarship has offered numerous alternative definitions of myth, difficulties in the use of the term remain. J. Rogerson, in his book *Myth in Old Testament Interpretation* (1974), examined how scholars used the term in different generations. He concludes that it is 'impossible and undesirable to find a single definition for the term' (p. 174). Nevertheless, despite the problems that arise from its use, the word myth is useful because it signals the unusual nature of the stories in Genesis 1–11. In these stories, serpents speak; heavenly beings take human wives; animals live together peacefully on a boat for many days; and humans attempt to build a tower that reaches to the heavens. Whatever one thinks of these narratives, one cannot deny their unusual nature. The characters featured in the story inhabit a world very different from our own. The word 'myth' signals this difference to us and prepares us for the type of stories contained in Genesis 1–11.

Creation and expulsion from Eden

The theme of creation stands at the centre of much Jewish and Christian theology. It occurs repeatedly in both the Old and New Testaments (see, for example, Job 38:4ff; Ps 8; John 1 etc.) and features as an important part of doctrinal and ethical debate. Consequently, the account of creation given by the book of Genesis has been interpreted in different ways and used to demonstrate a variety of distinct positions. Interpretations interested in identifying the historical background of the text, have generally concentrated on two major questions: the sources that lie behind the text and ancient Near Eastern parallels with it. Other interpretations have drawn insights from the texts on, among other things, anthropology and environmental issues.

The two accounts of creation

The first two chapters of Genesis describe the creation of the world. Out of chaos, a new world emerges by the word of God. However, a brief examination of the text indicates that Genesis 2 does not flow on easily from Genesis 1. Genesis 1 describes creation as taking place in two sets of three actions. C. Westermann (1988) calls the first set 'three separations' (p. 8) and the second set 'three quickenings' (p. 9). The first set lays the foundations of the earth and the second calls life forth from it. Each of the separations more or less matches one of the quickenings, as the table below illustrates.

Table 3: Separations and quickenings in Genesis 1

Day	Action	Day	Action
1	God separates **light** from **darkness**	4	God commands **lights** to hang in the sky
2	God separates the **sea** from the **sky**	5	God brings forth **sea creatures** and **birds**
3	God separates the **dry land** from the **sea**	6	God brings forth **animals** and creates **humankind**

However, when we reach Genesis 2 none of this is mentioned. Genesis 2:5 specifically says that no plants have yet been created, despite the fact that in 1:11 God commands the earth to produce plants and trees of all kinds. However, this account cannot even be seen as a repetition of Genesis 1, because in Genesis 1 humanity is created before the plants and trees but in Genesis 2, after them.

Another difference is that the Genesis 1 account is simply concerned with portraying how creation took place, whereas the account in Genesis 2 acts as a prologue for Genesis 3, where the fall and its consequences are described. Indeed, in this second account of creation, the act of creation seems subordinate in interest to the account of fall which immediately follows it. These two stories function in different ways. Another interesting contrast relates to differing attitudes to water. In Genesis 1, water is a chaotic, fearful substance which God separates and subdues (Gen 1:6–10); in Genesis 2 it is a life-giving substance needed for the act of creation itself (Gen 2:5–6). In one, water is feared; in the other, longed for. It is possible that this reflects different origins for the two stories. Genesis 1 may come from a background where floods were common and Genesis 2 from a culture where drought was experienced.

These differences indicate that Genesis 1 and 2 may have originated from two separate sources. Genesis 1 is widely regarded as having been written by the Priestly Writer and Genesis 2 by the Yahwist. The terminology, literary style and theology of each account support this opinion. Genesis 1 presents the account of creation almost as a list (day one, day two etc.), whereas Genesis 2 gives a much more flowing account of the events. In Genesis 1, God is a distant, transcendent being who commands and it is done. In Genesis 2, God seems more intimately involved with the act of creation, particularly in attempting to find a companion for Adam (see the discussion of the Documentary Hypothesis in Chapter 1, above, for further characteristics of each source).

Ancient Near Eastern parallels with the Genesis accounts of creation and fall

Scholars attempting to understand how the text of Genesis reached its current form have also turned to other texts from surrounding cultures for illumination. Despite the problems associated with the term myth, myths have been an important element in the study of the Hebrew Bible. Archaeological discoveries of the nineteenth and twentieth centuries brought to light the existence of numerous myths from elsewhere in the ancient Near East. The existence of other stories which attempt to describe the origins of the world is not surprising, as most cultures attempt to describe their origins in some way. What is remarkable about these texts is that they originate from a similar area and culture to the biblical accounts and, in certain respects, reflect a similar view of the world.

The 'ancient Near East' is a loose term used to describe various groups of peoples who lived in the area of land which stretches from the Mediterranean coast (modern Egypt in the south to modern Turkey in the north) to the east (modern Iran and Iraq). While parallels have been discovered in texts from all over the ancient Near East and beyond, the most striking are Sumerian, Akkadian, Babylonian, Egyptian and Ugaritic in origin. Sumerian, Akkadian and Babylonian texts all originate, at different times, from Mesopotamia, a region bounded by the river Euphrates and the river Tigris. Sumerian civilization is best known for its artwork and was at its peak from the third to the early second millennium BCE. The Sumerians were not Semitic and spoke 'Sumer', a language that died out in the second millennium BCE, although it continued as a written language for much longer. The Akkadians were a Semitic people whose power began to increase towards the end of the third millennium BCE. Their influence was replaced during the second millennium BCE by that of the Assyrians in northern Mesopotamia and the Babylonians in southern Mesopotamia.

To the west, the empire of Egypt produced various important texts. Texts from these major, well-known empires have long been recognized as containing material parallel to the narratives of the Pentateuch. The material of the ancient kingdom of Ugarit has only relatively recently been considered to contain parallels with the biblical material. Ugarit is on the Mediterranean coast of modern-day Syria and was the capital of the kingdom of Ugarit whose power was at its peak in the second millennium BCE. Many texts from this kingdom were discovered by archaeologists from 1929 onwards and their importance recognized.

While many of the myths from other ancient Near Eastern cultures are very different from the accounts in Genesis 1–11, some of them seem remarkably similar. This has led scholars to reflect upon the connection between the biblical accounts and the ancient Near Eastern texts. Similarities between the creation accounts of Genesis and those

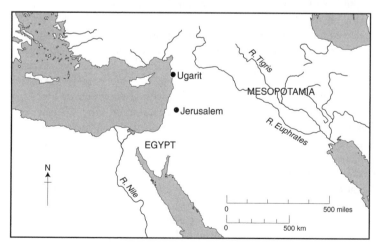

Map 1: The ancient Near Eastern world

of other ancient Near Eastern religions exist on many different levels. Some similarities concern the motifs contained within a story; others reflect a similar view of the world, the structure of the story or an underlying pattern. Many of the important ancient Near Eastern texts are published in J. B. Pritchard, *Ancient Near Eastern Texts Relating to the Old Testament* (1969) (normally abbreviated as *ANET*). Abbreviated sections of the most important texts are available in a more accessible form in V. H. Matthews and D. C. Benjamin, *Old Testament Parallels* (1991).

Three motifs found in the accounts of Genesis 2–3 have striking parallels with various ancient Near Eastern texts. Genesis 2 describes God forming Adam out of clay. This notion occurs in various ancient Near Eastern texts but the most remarkable is in the *Atrahasis Epic*. Here, the goddess Mami forms humans by pinching off pieces of clay (*ANET*, 99–100). The tree of life features briefly in Genesis 2–3. Although the focus of the narrative's attention is the tree of the knowledge of good and evil, the tree of life is mentioned in Genesis 2:9 and 3:24. The idea of 'living for ever' is one which features in many texts across the world, not simply those of the ancient Near East. Nevertheless, certain parallels do exist, particularly in texts which come from the Mesopotamian region. The *Myth of Adapa* is a story opposite to the one in Genesis 3. This myth tells the story of the first human being, to whom the gods offered the bread and water of life. Adapa, thinking that this was a trick, refused the food and drink. Consequently, he lost the chance of immortality. The *Gilgamesh Epic* tells of the efforts of the hero Gilgamesh to gain eternal life. After many adventures, he finally succeeded in acquiring a plant which offers the gift of rejuvenation. However, a snake ate the plant and was thus able to shed its skin repeatedly. Although both of these accounts present interesting perspectives on the question of immortality, neither bears much resemblance to the Genesis account, which is much more concerned with the sin of seeking knowledge than with seeking eternal life.

The serpent of Genesis 3 is a notable creature in other ancient Near Eastern texts. The *Gilgamesh Epic*, mentioned above, features a snake who consumed the rejuvenating plant. This story, however, does not explain the enmity between humanity and snakes; rather it explains why snakes are able to shed their skin. J. J. Scullion, in his article on the 'Genesis Narrative' in *The Anchor Bible Dictionary*, notes the serpents in Canaanite texts which represent fertility and those in Mesopotamian and Egyptian texts which represent either wisdom or magic (Scullion, 1992, pp. 941–56). Exodus 4, where the Lord turns Moses' staff into a snake to demonstrate his power, provides an interesting biblical comparison to this.

Many motifs in the Genesis accounts are similar to those in ancient Near Eastern texts. The ones mentioned above are simply the most striking. Another similarity exists in the realm of cosmology. Although the Genesis 1 account has a limited description of the structure of the world, enough information exists to note parallels with, for example, the structure of the world given in the Babylonian epic, *Enuma Elish*. The primary similarity is the belief in the existence of a firmament. Genesis 1:6–7 describes God separating the waters by means of a 'dome' (NRSV). The Hebrew word is more vague and literally means something beaten or stretched out (e.g. a thin piece of metal). This means that God hollowed out a space in the middle of dense waters, in which he later created the earth. The waters flowed above the sky and under the earth but between them a space existed. A similar idea exists in the *Enuma Elish*. Here Marduk, after conquering the goddess Tiamat, cuts her body in two and used half to form the sky and half to form the earth. This sealed out the waters of Apsu. Here again is the idea that before creation nothing but water existed. The creative act hollowed out a space in the waters for life to exist.

This is not the only similarity between Genesis 1 and the *Enuma Elish*. Another striking parallel is the order of creation. Genesis 1 gives the order of creation as the creation of light; the separation between the waters; the creation of dry ground; the placing of the sun, moon and stars in the sky; the creation of sea creatures; and finally the creation of animals and humans. The *Enuma Elish* presents a similar order of creation, culminating in the creation of human beings. However, unlike Genesis 1, it does not split each of these acts into periods of time.

The area of similarity between Genesis and other ancient Near Eastern texts which has most interested scholars is the idea of creation taking place through God's conflict with chaos and the dragon. At the end of the nineteenth century, Gunkel wrote a book entitled *Schöpfung und Chaos in Urzeit und Endzeit*, which means 'Creation and Chaos in Primeval Times and End Times'. This book was influential but unfortunately was never translated into English. The significance of Gunkel's book was that he encouraged the use of extra-biblical texts, such as myths from Mesopotamia, to understand the biblical narrative. In particular, he proposed that the conflict between the god Marduk and the goddess Tiamat, described in the *Enuma Elish*, stands behind many of the biblical accounts of creation. In the *Enuma Elish* this conflict took place immediately before creation. The story tells that the goddess Tiamat sought to kill the gods responsible for the death of her consort, Apsu. The gods, fearing the power of Tiamat, found a champion in Marduk, who engages in battle against her. In the course of the battle, Tiamat disguised herself as a dragon but was defeated and killed by Marduk, who used her body to form the sky and earth, as mentioned above.

While there is no mention of conflict with dragons in the Genesis accounts of creation, Gunkel pointed to other biblical texts, particularly in the Psalms and Job, as possible parallels with this tradition. He suggested that verses like Psalm 74:13–14,

> You divided the sea by your might;
>   you broke the heads of the dragons in the waters.
> You crushed the heads of Leviathan;
>   you gave him as food for the creatures of the wilderness.

might reflect a similar tradition (for other examples see Ps 89:10; Job 9:8). As regards the Genesis account, although it does not recount God in conflict with the dragon like these other texts, it does speak of God dominating the waters. Indeed, Gunkel pointed out that the Hebrew word *tehom*, translated waters or deep, is cognate with the word *Tiamat* and might reflect a connection.

Recent archaeological finds in the city of Ugarit have lead various scholars, most notably J. Day, to propose that the background for this tradition of conflict with a dragon is not Mesopotamian but Canaanite. In his book, *God's Conflict with the Dragon and the Sea* (1985), Day argues persuasively that myths about Ba'al's conflict with Yam (told in other forms as a conflict with Leviathan) are a more likely background for the biblical narrative.

The similarities of motif, cosmology, the order of creation and the myth of conflict with a dragon must lead us to reflect upon their significance. Gunkel and his followers concluded that Genesis 1 is indebted in some way to the *Enuma Elish* account, although the functions of the texts are different. More recent scholars, such as W. G. Lambert (1965), have concluded that the similarities may reflect not direct borrowing but simply a similar view of the world. Whatever the reason for these similarities, one cannot fail to notice the differences that also exist. The most notable difference is the absolute power of God in the biblical texts. Unlike the ancient Near Eastern narratives, in Genesis victory by God is never doubted. In the *Enuma Elish* creation takes place as a by-product of warfare between the gods; in Genesis the creation of the world was the focus of the whole account. In the Genesis account the peace and orderliness of creation contrast starkly with the chaos of the *Enuma Elish* account. While the authors of the Genesis accounts may have known of the other ancient Near Eastern accounts of creation, their view of God is radically different.

Literary, feminist and environmental interpretations of Genesis 1–3

The interpretations of Genesis 1–3 discussed so far in this chapter have both been concerned to understand more about the origins of the text. Other interpretations seek to understand more about the texts' view of God, humanity and the environment. J. Goldingay (1998) presents an unusual reading of the narrative. In a creative reading told from the perspective of Eve, Goldingay questions the traditional understanding of the divine prohibition to eat from the tree of the knowledge of good and evil. Goldingay points out that the punishment promised upon eating the fruit of the tree, that Adam and Eve would die, did not happen. It did not even happen in the near future, because Adam lived to be 930 years old. Instead, he suggests that the prohibition was a test similar to that given to Abraham over the sacrifice of Isaac, intended to teach the recipients more about God and their relationship with God, the difference being that Abraham learnt his lesson through obedience and Adam through disobedience.

Genesis 1–3 has long stood at the centre of the debate about the nature of men and women and their relationship throughout history. As early as the New Testament, the author of the first epistle to Timothy (2:13–14) cites Genesis 2–3 as the reason for women's inability to have authority over men. This portrayal of woman as subordinate to man is often contrasted with Genesis 1:27, which states that both male and female were created in the image of God. H. Schüngel-Straumann (1993) presented a helpful survey of the history of interpretation of both passages, showing how even Genesis 1 has been used in what she calls 'anti-woman' arguments (p. 64).

Unsurprisingly, many interpretations have been put forward which reflect upon the significance of gender in the Genesis accounts. The best-known interpretation of this sort was put forward by P. Trible (1978). Trible argued that the problem with Genesis 2–3 is not so much the text itself as the subsequent interpretations of the text. She calls the narrative 'A Love Story Gone Awry' (pp. 72–143) and her interpretation pivots on the Hebrew pun in Genesis 2:7. Here the man (Hebrew 'adam) is formed from the earth (Hebrew 'adamah). Trible maintains that this pun is deliberate and that 'man' here should be translated 'earth-creature' (p. 77). Only after woman was created did the 'adam gain sexual identity. The story is a love story gone awry because in the fall their initial unity is separated:

> By betraying the woman to God, the man opposed himself to her; by ignoring him in her reply to God, the woman separates herself from the man. (p. 120)

The result of this, Trible maintains, is a 'hierarchy of division (p. 128). Trible's close reading of the text, though not always accepted, is widely recognized as a significant attempt to approach the text with new eyes.

Trible maintains that the problem for women lay not in Genesis but in subsequent misogynist interpretations of it. In contrast, D. Jobling maintains that the problem lay in the text itself. Life in the Garden of Eden has traditionally been viewed as an idyllic existence in paradise. Against this view, Jobling (1986) argues that Genesis 2–3 was instead an account of the hardships of life in the Garden of Eden. Unlike the outside world, agriculture was the only pursuit available and inside the garden woman the only company. The function of this story, therefore, was to encourage men to cope with the harshness of life outside Eden by showing them that life inside the garden had its own disadvantages. A rallying cry of a different kind is identified by C. Meyers (1988). Like Jobling, she is interested in the climate which produced the text and maintains that the Genesis 3 passage reflects the situation in Israel in the Iron Age I period. The context she paints for this passage is of settlement in the Palestinian hill country. Life at this time consisted of hard agricultural labour and required maximum commitment from both men and women. She maintains that the gender roles painted by Genesis 3 arise within this context and should be understood as such.

N. Lohfink (1994) concentrates not on the relationship between women and men but on the relationship between humanity and the world. The first chapter of his book, *Theology of the Pentateuch*, considers the command in Genesis 1:28 to 'subdue the earth'. He criticizes certain readings of the text which support exploitation of the world's resources. Instead, he maintains, Genesis 1:28 should be read in the light of the Priestly Writer's understanding of 'artistic and technical achievement' (p. 16) as set out in Exodus 25–31 and 35–40. The command to build and furnish the sanctuary, which these chapters contain, seems to continue the divine act of creation in Genesis 1. In the light of this and of humanity's creation 'in the image of God', Lohfink concludes that the command in Genesis 1:28 was 'so that the earth may be developed to resemble heaven, in order that the earth may become the dwelling place of God' (p. 17). Far from supporting the exploitation of the earth, this verse encourages the transformation of earth into a heavenly dwelling place.

Cain and Abel

The story which immediately follows Adam and Eve's expulsion from the Garden of Eden centres upon their offspring – Cain and Abel. This well-known story presents an account of the first murder. Cain's feeling of rejection, after God declined his sacrifice, caused him to kill his brother Abel. The New Testament interprets this passage as presenting inherent 'righteousness' on Abel's part and inherent 'evil' on Cain's part (Matt 23:35; 1 John 3:12). The epistle to the Hebrews even goes so far as to say that Abel's sacrifice was accepted because he made it 'by faith' (Heb 11:4). Unfortunately, the text of Genesis 4 is not as clear as this. No reason is given for the acceptance of Abel's sacrifice and the rejection of Cain's.

G. Wenham (1987, p. 104) enunciates five possible reasons for this: three concern God's attitude, two that of Cain and Abel. The first possibility is that God prefers shepherds (Abel) to gardeners (Cain); the second that God prefers animal to grain sacrifices; and the third that God's actions are inscrutable and the choice simply reflects the mystery of divine election. Of the final two possibilities, one refers to Hebrews 11:4 as the solution and the other proposes that the difference was one of quality: Abel produced the finest from his flock; Cain just 'an offering of the fruit of the ground'. Whatever the reason for God's choice of one sacrifice over the other, this is not the central focus of the story (although in many interpretations it has become the central focus). Instead, the narrative focuses upon Cain's response to the rejection of his sacrifice. It is this response that defines Cain's sin, not the nature of his sacrifice.

In an article published in 1990, G. West contrasted two liberationist readings of the story from South Africa. Both were interested in the conflict presented by the narrative, though one saw it as a support for the oppressed and the other as a support for the oppressor. A. Boesak reads the story as an account of struggle from a situation of struggle. His interest in the story is to identify an analogy with his present situation and his understanding of the narrative is that it maintains that there is no place for oppression in God's world. God unequivocally condemns Cain for his act of oppression in murdering Abel. In contrast, I. Mosala, while also writing from a 'situation of struggle', was more interested in the historical background of the narrative. Historical critics have long recognized, within the narrative of Cain and Abel, a reference to the tension that existed in the ancient world between nomads and settled farmers. Abel, a sheep farmer, represented the nomads and Cain, a tiller of the land, a settled farmer. Mosala maintained that the narrative supported the eviction of the settled farmers from their land: Cain, the settled farmer, sinned against Abel, his nomadic brother, and was forced to leave his land and wander over the face of the earth. This, Mosala argued, 'inaugurated a relentless process of land dispossession of the village peasants in Israel' (cited in West, p. 307). Mosala also noted that this account is attributed to the 'J' source, reputedly written during the monarchical period and thus, he maintained, supporting the rights of the élite over the village peasants. These contrasting views of the narrative illustrate well the differences that can emerge in interpretations of the same text: Boesak views the story as a condemnation of oppression; Mosala as supporting it.

Genealogies

Genealogies appear regularly throughout Genesis 1–11. Their value is twofold. On the one hand, they allow the authors of the narrative to cover large periods of time without giving a detailed description of the events. On the other hand, they show how the ancient characters that feature in the story are related to the stories' original readers. This second feature of the genealogies allows the readers of the narrative to identify what happened as a story of their own 'beginnings'. This was continued by the New Testament writers, particularly Matthew and Luke (Matt 1:1–16; Luke 3:23–38), who used the technique of genealogies to tie Christianity to its roots within Ancient Israel.

A detailed consideration of the genealogies contained in Genesis 1–11 indicates that there are two different ways of presenting genealogical type material (this material includes both 'straight genealogies' and the table of nations found in chapter 10). The first type of genealogy (4:17–26; 10:8–19, 24–30) contains a certain amount of narrative and explains the origins of certain peoples (10:10), occupations (4:19–22;) and sayings (10:9). The other type of genealogy in Genesis (5; 10:1–7, 20–23, 32; 11:10–32) seems to be more of a list of names and, in the case of Genesis 5, is interested in recounting the ages of the people recorded. Source critics generally attribute the first, more narrative style of genealogy to 'J' and the second, more list-like style, to 'P'. Indeed, scholars such as von Rad ([1956] 1972) maintain that the Hebrew word *toledot* (translated by the NRSV as 'descendants'), which occurs in Genesis 5:1; 6:9; 10:1 and 11:10, indicates that 'P' borrowed from an ancient 'toledoth book' (p. 70) in setting out his genealogies.

One interesting ancient interpretation of the biblical text focuses on the figure of Enoch, mentioned in Genesis 4:17–18 as the son of Cain and in Genesis 5:21–24 as the father of Methuselah. The phrase 'Enoch walked with God; then he was no more, because God took him' (Gen 5:24) seems to have given rise to certain traditions about him. Ethiopic Enoch (often called 1 Enoch) and Slavonic Enoch (often called 2 Enoch) contain extended speculations about Enoch's ascent into heaven and his role in the heavenly realms. A third work, *Sepher Hekhalot* (often called 3 Enoch) also contains Enochic tradition but focuses primarily on the ascent to heaven of another figure, Rabbi Ishmael.

Translations of these works can be found in J. H. Charlesworth (1983), *The Old Testament Pseudepigrapha*, vol 1, pp. 5–315, under the titles 1, 2 and 3 Enoch. The importance of these speculations is highlighted by the fact that an Aramaic version of Ethiopic Enoch was discovered at Qumran and that the New Testament epistle of Jude (vv. 14–15) gives a citation from the book as though citing from scripture.

The sons of God and the daughters of humans

Between the genealogy of Genesis 5 and the flood narrative stands a brief yet strange account of the union between the sons of God and the daughters of humans (Gen 6:3–4). The narrative is surprising on numerous levels. Although the 'sons of God' do appear elsewhere in the Old Testament, most notably in Job 1:6ff., their appearance is sufficiently rare to be unusual. In addition the narrative seems to have a double purpose. Verse 3 stresses that, despite union with the sons of God, humanity is mortal and will not live for ever. Verse 4 uses the account to explain the presence of the Nephilim, giants with great power who appear again in Numbers 13:33 and Deuteronomy 2:10–11. Indeed, verse 4 provides a puzzle of its own. The origins of the Nephilim are traced to a time before the flood; the account does not explain how they survived the flood to be present 'also afterward' (v. 4).

The account seems to be reminiscent of myths from other cultures where gods and humans produce powerful offspring, and yet no accounts are sufficiently close to suggest any influence upon the biblical narrative. Perhaps the best explanation for the inclusion of the narrative is, like the creation accounts, to point to the differences between the Genesis tradition and other ancient Near Eastern texts. Elsewhere unions between gods and humans produce superhuman powers; here, verse 3 makes very clear that immortality did not result from the union. In the overall flow of the narrative from Genesis 1–11, a further boundary has been broken. In forming a union with the daughters of humans, the sons of God have broken the bounds between heaven and earth set down in Genesis 1.

Like the cryptic verse of Genesis 5:21–24, this narrative has become the subject of extensive speculation in Ethiopic Enoch. The first section of this lengthy work is known as 'the book of the Watchers' and concerns the fate of those 'angels' or 'watchers' who broke the boundary between heaven and earth as described in Genesis 6:1–4. The book of the Watchers contains more than one tradition about the actions of the fallen angels. The basic tradition reflected in the biblical narrative is associated with the figure of Semyaz and his followers. A second tradition also exists alongside this one which asserts that it was Azaz'el and his followers teaching the people divine secrets who were responsible for the fall of the Watchers. The account of the fall given in Ethiopic Enoch is much longer than that in Genesis 6:1–4. As a result, most scholars regard the Enochic account as being a later expansion of the original narrative. J. T. Milik (1976, pp. 22–41) has proposed, however, that the opposite is the case. In other words, he argues that the Enoch tradition is earlier than that of Genesis and that the Genesis account is a conflation of the older Enoch account.

Flood accounts

Genesis 6:5 begins an extended account of God's punishment of the world by a flood. Verse 6 states that God 'was sorry that he had made humankind on the earth' (NRSV) and resolved to undo his creative act. The flood, if viewed from the cosmology suggested by Genesis 1, is in fact a great act of 'un-creation'. In creation, God gradually separated out a space in the midst of the waters, in which humankind could live and multiply. In the flood, God filled in that space once more. The waters above and below the earth flowed back to where they had been before God separated them. If creation had been the imposition of order on chaos, the flood was the imposition of chaos on order. Nevertheless, the world does not remain in an uncreated state. In a cycle, identified by D. J. A. Clines (1997, pp. 80–2) as the Creation–Uncreation–Recreation theme, at the end of the flood the waters are separated once more, the command to multiply is reissued and order over chaos returns.

The two accounts of flood

Just as scholars identified two different accounts of creation in Genesis 1–2, so also they have pointed out the presence of two sources behind the flood narratives. Unlike the creation accounts, however, the two sources behind the flood account are not placed side by side in the text, with one beginning where the other ends. Instead, the accounts seem to be interwoven in the same narrative. While the flood narrative has a single overarching structure, different details stand next to each other in the flow of the story. For example, in Genesis 6:19–20, Noah is commanded to take two of each species of animal into the ark; in Genesis 6:2–3, he is commanded to take seven pairs of clean animals and one pair of unclean animals into the ark. Such discrepancies seem to indicate the presence of two separate accounts woven together to make a single one. In this case, the task of the source critic is made more complex by the fact that not all details are contained in both accounts. The task of 'unravelling' the narrative into its two constituent parts requires close attention to the style, theology and terminology of the text. The complexity of the task means that, although there is a consensus about the sources of large portions of the narrative, there is no such consensus about smaller sub-sections of verses. The division of the account given in the table below is drawn from C. Westermann (1988, pp. 45–50).

Table 4: The 'P' and 'J' elements of the flood narrative

'P'		J	
Title and Introduction	6:9–10		
Divine punishment of human wickedness	6:11–13	Divine punishment of human wickedness	6:5–8
Noah commanded to build an ark	6:14–18a		
Noah commanded to take his family and two of every species into the ark	6:18b–22	Noah commanded to take his household, seven pairs of clean and one pair of each unclean animal into the ark	7:1-5
Age of Noah	7:6		
Date of flood	7:11		
		Rain falls for 40 days	7:12
Noah, his family and animals went into the ark	7:13–16a	Noah, his family and animals went into the ark	7:7–10
Flood comes on the earth	7:17a	Flood comes on the earth	7:16b and 17b
Description of flood	7:18–21	Description of flood	7:22–23
Flood lasts 150 days	7:24		
God stops flood	8:1–2a	Flood stops	8:2b–3a
Waters recede and ark stops on Ararat	8:3b–5	Noah sends out birds to test the level of the waters	8:6–12
Date for drying up of the flood	8:13a and 14a	Noah sees that the earth is dry	8:13b
Noah is commanded to leave the ark	8:15–19		
		Noah sacrifices to God	8:20–22
God makes a covenant with Noah	9:1–17		
Length of Noah's life	9:28–29		

This type of breakdown of the text reveals various points. The first is that, although there is repetition between the verses attributed to 'P' and those attributed to 'J', we do not have two complete interwoven flood narratives. At various points, the 'J' narrative does not contain certain vital parts of the story, such as the building of the ark or Noah leaving the ark. In these instances, the reader must rely on the 'P' account for the narrative to make sense. Another point of interest is that the narrative is punctuated with verses which date the events described (indicated in the table by italics) but sometimes seem to interrupt the flow of the account.

This evidence raises questions about the process by which the sources became joined within the Pentateuch. One option is that a later independent redactor joined an original 'P' source and an original 'J' source. Wellhausen (1885) accounted for the dominance of the 'P' source on the grounds that it is as if 'P' 'were the scarlet thread upon which the pearls of JE were hung' (p. 332). However, various scholars have also cited this evidence in their alteration of the basic Documentary Hypothesis. Two scholars who have found support for their theories in the flood narrative are F. M. Cross and J. Blenkinsopp. Cross (1973) points out that the flood narrative was one of only four Priestly narratives in Genesis (the other three being the creation, the description of a covenant with Abraham and the purchase of the Cave of Machpela). He maintains that the 'P' account of the flood is 'not the work of a redactor juxtaposing blocks of material, but that of a tradent reworking and supplementing a traditional story' (p. 303). What Cross's account does not explain is why certain vital elements of the 'J' account were omitted, nor why 'P' saw fit to supplement the account with certain additional, contradictory sections. Blenkinsopp uses the same evidence to argue an opposing position. He proposes that 'J' is not the narrative basis for 'P' but a 'later expansion and commentary' on the original 'P' source (Blenkinsopp, 1992, p. 78). Again, however, he does not explain why such an expansion should contain such contradictory material.

Ancient Near Eastern parallels with the flood narratives

The accounts of creation contained certain striking parallels with myths from other ancient Near Eastern civilizations. The flood narratives contain even more parallels with accounts from neighbouring countries. Accounts of flood are far from being unique to the book of Genesis, but those closest to the biblical accounts originate from the region of Mesopotamia. The accounts exist in various languages (the most important being Sumerian, Akkadian and Assyrian), with various heroes (including Utnapishtim, Atrahasis and Ziusudra) and in various degrees of completeness. The most complete version of the narrative is the *Gilgamesh Epic*, though it may well have drawn its flood narrative from its more ancient companion, the *Atrahasis Epic*.

The *Gilgamesh Epic* has been reconstructed from various different versions in different periods, the most complete coming from the Old Babylonian period (1750–1600 BCE) and the Neo-Assyrian period (750–612 BCE). A detailed discussion of the text, its sources and origins, is given by J. M. Sasson in his article, 'The Gilgamesh Epic', in The *Anchor Bible Dictionary*, vol II, pp. 1024–7. The account records the actions of the semi-divine king Gilgamesh, who, the story recounts, ruled in southern Mesopotamia in the third millennium BCE. The account contains a long description of the acts of Gilgamesh and his friend Enkidu. At the end of the narrative, though probably not original to it, Gilgamesh found Utnapishtim, who recounted to Gilgamesh how he, Utnapishtim, achieved immortality.

This immortality was granted to Utnapishtim after he was saved from a universal flood, by which the gods intended to annihilate the earth. The general pattern of the narrative bears a remarkable resemblance to the Genesis account (English versions can be found in *ANET*, 93–5, and Matthews and Benjamin, 1991, pp. 35–40). The god Enlil decided to flood the earth. Warned by the god Ea, Utnapishtim tore down his house and built a cube-shaped ship, into which he took treasure, his family and both domestic and wild beasts. The storm raged for six days. On the seventh day the storm died down and the ark came to rest on Mount Nisir. The ship was grounded for six days. On the seventh day, Utnapishtim sent out a dove, which returned to him because she found no resting-place. Then he sent out a swallow, which also came back. Finally, he sent a raven, which did not return. At this point, Utnapishtim released the creatures from the ark and sacrificed to the gods. When they 'smelled the sweet savour. The gods crowded like flies about the sacrifice' (lines 160–1). When the god Enlil saw that Utnapishtim had survived the flood, he was angry because he had intended to destroy all humanity. In order to preserve his plan, he made Utnapishtim and his wife divine and hence immortal.

The flood narrative in the *Gilgamesh Epic* is very close to that of the *Atrahasis Epic* and may have been draw from it. Various additional details contained in the *Atrahasis Epic* are worthy of comment. The flood narrative in the *Atrahasis Epic* occurs in the context of a primeval history, after a description of creation. The reason given for the flood is that there was a population explosion and the noise of humanity began to disturb the gods. In this account, after the flood, Anu (the leader of the gods) solved the population problem by making some women infertile, some babies die and some women priestesses, who must be celibate.

The parallels between these accounts and the biblical accounts are obvious. Motifs such as the choosing of one person to survive the flood, the building of an ark, the preservation of his family and some animals, the sending out of different birds at the end of the flood, all bear a certain resemblance to the biblical account. One of the most striking parallels is the reaction of the gods to the sacrifice after the flood. In both the *Gilgamesh Epic* and the *Atrahasis Epic* the gods smelled the sweet aroma of the sacrifice; in Genesis 8:21 we are told that 'the Lord smelled the pleasing odour' of the sacrifice. Such parallels between the accounts indicate that, at the very least, the biblical authors were aware of traditions about the flood also known by the Mesopotamian authors. Nevertheless, as was the case with the parallels between the creation accounts and the ancient Near Eastern myths, significant differences between the accounts indicate a very different view of God's relationship with the world.

In the *Atrahasis Epic*, the leader of the gods, Anu, decided to destroy humanity because their noise was disturbing the gods. In both the *Atrahasis Epic* and the *Gilgamesh Epic*, the hero is warned of the flood by one god at odds with the god who wishes to destroy the earth. In Genesis, humanity plays a much more important part in the narrative. It is God's attempt to undo the sin of humankind that causes the flood and God's mercy that leads to the saving of Noah. While the biblical writers may have known of similar accounts about the flood, their purpose in writing was very different.

The theme of covenant and the Priestly Writer

God's making of a covenant with Noah at the end of the flood account is, according to source critics, to be attributed to the Priestly Source. This theme of covenant has long been regarded as a defining element of the 'P' tradition. Wellhausen noted four major periods of history: the ages of Adam, Noah, Abraham and Moses, each marked by a covenant. As Cross notes, it has regularly been recognized that God did not make a covenant with Adam (Cross, 1973, p. 294) but he did receive a blessing, which was also given to Noah, Abraham and Moses, as the table opposite illustrates.

The significance of this blessing formula is increased by the fact that God did not make an initial covenant with Adam. The use of a similar formula in subsequent covenants marks a return to the original blessing given to humanity in creation. The covenants made with Noah, Abraham and Moses all signalled the possibility of a return to the ideal

Table 5: The blessings given to Adam, Noah, Abraham and Moses

Name	Reference	Content of Blessing
Adam	Genesis 1:28	God blessed them, and God said to them, 'Be fruitful and multiply, and fill the earth and subdue it; and have dominion over the fish of the sea and over the birds of the air and over every living thing that moves upon the earth.'
Noah	Genesis 9:7	'And you, be fruitful and multiply, abound on the earth and multiply in it.'
Abraham	Genesis 17:6	'I will make you exceedingly fruitful; and I will make nations of you, and kings shall come from you.'
Moses	Leviticus 26:9	'I will look with favour upon you and make you fruitful and multiply you; and I will maintain my covenant with you.'

state at creation. A sign accompanied each covenant: these were a rainbow, circumcision and Sabbath observance respectively. Cross also notes that each age after Adam is separated from the one that follows by an upheaval of some sort: the flood separates the age of Noah from Adam, the migration of Terah and Abraham separates Abraham from Noah and the exodus separates Moses from the Patriarchs. These include a removal from and resettlement in a land. Even Noah's upheaval involves a removal from the land and subsequent resettlement in it. The blessing formula, which commands the recipient to be fruitful and multiply in the newly settled land, stresses this point.

Each covenant in each subsequent age became 'deeper and narrower', in that more was revealed to fewer people (Cross, 1973, p. 296). An example of this is the divine name revealed as *'elohim* to Noah, *'el Shaddai* to Abraham and YHWH to Moses. As the covenants narrowed, from righteous humanity as a whole to Moses as the leader of the people of Israel, so also more of God's nature was revealed. The final covenant with Moses and the people of Israel also involved extensive regulations for both worship and the everyday lives of the Israelites. These, according to Cross, were the means by which the transcendent and holy God was able to walk among the sinful people. This is reflected by the regular use of the Hebrew root *skn*, from which the word *shekinah* comes, which means literally 'to tent' or 'to live the life of the tent dweller' (p. 299). As Cross regards the Priestly Writer as the final creative redactor of the Pentateuch, this point receives even greater emphasis. According to him, the Priestly Writer was the dynamic 'author' of the Pentateuch, who drew together many existing sources, including 'JE'. In the light of this, 'P's' frequent use of the root *skn* becomes even more significant. If 'P' knew of the 'J' tradition of YHWH walking with Adam and Eve in the cool of the evening, then regular reference to God dwelling with God's people points backwards, as the blessing formulae do, to an idyllic situation immediately after creation took place.

Noah the vintner

The flood narrative is concluded with the rather surprising account of Noah's drunkenness (9:20–27). The account does not indicate what was so sinful about Ham's action and is made more confusing by the fact that although Ham is the one who sins against his father, it is Canaan, Ham's son, who is cursed by Noah. Scholars such as Westermann (1987, pp. 68–9) account for this confusion by maintaining that the account consists of two originally separate traditions: one which has the sons of Noah as Ham, Shem and Japheth, and another which contains the curse of Canaan and blessing of Shem and Japheth. The poetic form of this curse indicates that it may have been a well-known formula, explaining the oppression of the descendants of Canaan, the Canaanites, by the descendants of Shem, the Israelites. The short narrative of Ham's sin, however confusing, gives this curse a narrative framework and additional justification.

The tower of Babel

The narrative of the primeval history ends with the account of the attempt to build a tower as far as the heavens. In Genesis 6:1–4 the bounds of heaven were broken by the sons of God forming unions with the daughters of humans. Here the sin is made even greater by a human attempt to storm the heavenly realms by the building of a tower. Various attempts have been made to understand the origins of this story. Somewhat surprisingly, there are no immediate ancient Near Eastern parallels to the narrative, although Westermann refers to an African story which ends in the destruction of a building but no dispersal of languages (Westermann, 1988, p. 80).

The solution adopted by many scholars is that this is a polemic against the Babylonians. The Hebrew text engages in a play on words, maintaining that the name 'Babel' was due to its connection to the Hebrew verb *bll*, which means 'confuse'. Both literary and archae-ological evidence indicates that Babylon had many towers. The *Enuma Elish*, referred to above, celebrates the building of the Esagil, a

Babylonian temple and it was a common belief in Babylon that the top of temples reached as far as heaven. In additional to this, archaeological evidence points to the existence of many ziggurats in Mesopotamia, which were pyramid-type towers. Indeed, some have suggested a connection with the Entemenaki Temple, which was begun in the reign of Nebuchadnezzar but not completed until a long time afterwards (Rogerson, 1991, p. 76). The story seems to be ironic. Even though the humans intend to build the tower as far as heaven, God is forced to come down from heaven to see it. The purpose of the story, therefore, seems to be to deride human attempts to reach heaven, particularly those of the apparently all-powerful Babylonians. As far as the overall structure of Genesis is concerned, this is the ultimate breaking of the boundaries set down by God in the creative order: human arrogance has reached so far that it now even attempts to invade heaven. Von Rad ([1956] 1972, p. 153) noted that the account of the tower of Babel was the only account in Genesis 1–11 which does not contain a mitigation of God's initial curse. As a result, the primeval history ends by asking whether God's mercy has been exhausted.

Concluding remarks

The primeval history of Genesis 1–11 ends with a genealogy, which narrows down the focus of the story from the whole of humanity to Abraham, the father of the Israelites. Genesis 11 ends with the account of Terah, Abraham's father, moving from Ur to Haran. Thus the attention of the reader switches from universal history to family history, from the world to one particular figure, Abraham. The future for the whole of humanity may be a little bleak but we are now about to enter a new era, an era that turns the attention to the beginnings of Israel. The 'story of beginnings', which began with Adam in a period of universal history, is at an end, with the confusion of languages; a new period is about to begin with Abraham.

4

Go from your country ...

Genesis 12–50: Journeying to a new land

In Genesis 11, the story of the world's beginnings ends in the city of Babel, where language and culture become fragmented. The remainder of chapter 11 narrows the focus from the whole of humanity scattered over the face of the earth to the fate of one family, who live in the Mesopotamian region. Like those who attempted to build a tower into the heavens, Abraham and his family left their home in Mesopotamia at the instigation of God. Unlike those scattered across the face of the earth, their leaving involved a blessing, not a punishment, and began a new phase in our story of beginnings. Genesis 12–50 turns its attention away from the whole of humanity to one particular group of people, the family and descendants of Abraham. For the first time in the narrative so far, the beginnings of Israel become the focus of the narrative. Although the nature of the story is different, there are parallels between Genesis 1 and Genesis 11–12: just as the divine command called the world into being, so also the divine command calls Abraham to move to Canaan. For the first readers of this account, creation symbolized a movement from chaos to order, and a journey from Mesopotamia to Canaan would have symbolized a similar movement. The narrative of Genesis 12–50 follows the descendants of Abraham in their journey around the western reaches of the ancient Near East and leaves them in Egypt, where the book of Exodus begins.

Roughly speaking, Genesis 12–50 falls into three sections, each focusing on particular members of the same family. Genesis 12:1–25:18 (often called the Abraham cycle) features the events surrounding the life of Abraham, his wife Sarah, his nephew Lot and his sons Ishmael and Isaac. One of the central concerns of this section of the narrative is the production of a suitable heir for Abraham. This heir will inherit not only the usual property but also the promise of God made to Abraham to be the 'father of many nations'. Genesis 25:19–35:29 (often called the Jacob cycle) turns its attention to Abraham's twin grandchildren, Jacob and Esau, and their conflict, which is only resolved towards the end of this section (Genesis 33:1–20). The final section, Genesis 37–50, (often called the Joseph narrative) deals with Joseph, one of Jacob's twelve children, and his experiences in a foreign land.

These three sections, therefore, fashion their stories around three major characters, Abraham, Jacob and Joseph, and around three major themes, the continuity of a line, fraternal conflict and isolation in exile. As well as describing the lives of significant ancestors of old (called by many the Patriarchs), they explore central themes in the life of all societies: continuity, conflict and exile. This emphasizes the role of these stories as a mirror as well as a window. As a window, the text gives us as a glimpse into the lives and concerns of ancient ancestors; as a mirror, it reflects issues pertinent to many peoples' lives. This dual function ensures that this most ancient of narratives is at the same time the most contemporary.

The Patriarchs and historicity

As mentioned above, Genesis 12 begins a story of a different quality to those in Genesis 1–11. Attention has moved away from a universal story of earliest times to a particular family history. This concentration on the lives of a few individuals allows the account to provide a much more detailed insight into the way in which they lived their lives. This has inspired many scholars to attempt to locate Abraham and his descendants in a particular culture and time. The narrative indicates that Abraham and his descendants lived in the second millennium BCE and had a semi-nomadic lifestyle. They were not nomads in the sense of Bedouin tribes, who constantly move from place to place. Instead, they moved from one settled existence (in the city of Ur) to other settled existences in the land of Canaan, as the map overleaf illustrates.

The origins of the text

Source critics regard 'J', 'E' and 'P' as the major sources that lie behind Genesis 12–50. As far as a consensus can be said to exist, many scholars regard the text as either made up of these three sources, or of the two sources 'J' and 'E' edited by 'P'. However, more important than an examination of the written sources that lie behind the text has been an examination of its oral sources. As mentioned in Chapter 2, H. Gunkel accepted the general principles of the Documentary Hypothesis but believed that it was also possible to identify stages in the development

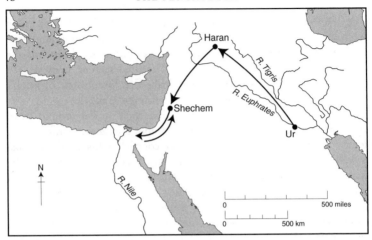

Map 2: Abraham's journey

of a text before it reached a written form. He identified units of varying lengths within the text which, he believed, could be traced back to oral tradition.

In his 1984 article, J. J. Scullion argued for a re-evaluation of the different 'labels' used for Old Testament narratives. As regards the smaller units of narrative in Genesis 12–50, he considers the terms 'legend' and 'story' to be the most useful. 'Legends' are those units of narrative, normally attached to a place, which explain how they came to be regarded as sacred. Under this definition, the account of Jacob's dream at Bethel (28:10–20) is a good example of 'legend'. 'Story' can be used of either long cycles of narrative, such as those about Abraham (11:27–25:18), Jacob (25:19–35:29) and Joseph (37–50), or of much shorter narratives such as the story about Abraham, Sarah and Hagar (16:1–16). In addition to 'story' for long cycles of narrative he also proposes the use of the term 'novella', which he regards as an appropriate description of the Joseph story (though not of any others in Genesis 12–50). He rejects Gunkel's term 'saga' as an appropriate description of the collection of stories about Abraham, Jacob and Joseph respectively, in favour of the term 'cycle'.

Whatever one chooses to call the narratives in Genesis 12–50, the brief description above indicates that scholars regard the stories of Genesis as containing two distinct stages: small individual units and larger collections of those units. The stages of oral tradition which lie behind the text almost inevitably consist of more than one layer: the initial 'independent' unit and the later collection of narratives. Scholars such as M. Noth, who built on Gunkel's work, became interested in the process that resulted in the collection of the independent units in a chronological order. This approach is known as 'tradition criticism' or the 'history of traditions'. As a historian, Noth was concerned to trace how the units of text were gathered into chains of narrative in the written text. Working on the premise that the units were originally independent, he argued that they reached a final 'chronological' form at the time of what he termed the 'amphictyony'. This theory, adopted from models in Classics, argued that Israel consisted of numerous tribes who came together in a federation, or amphictyony. These tribes brought with them traditions about their history which, under their common bond of the worship of YHWH, were joined to make a single tradition (a fuller account of Noth's theory of amphictyony can be found in M. Mills, 1999, pp. 26–8). G. von Rad was similarly interested in how the 'separate' traditions were joined together, but he regarded this as a literary, not historical, phenomenon. In other words, he considered that the traditions were joined together by the creative act of the Yahwist Writer, not during the amphictyony.

The notion that Abraham, Isaac and Jacob were not originally related, but that the stories about them were independent traditions about different ancestors which were joined later, became widespread among scholars. Scholars such as B. W. Anderson, in his classic work, *The Living World of the Old Testament* (1971), even maintained that the three major Patriarchs were connected with different geographical locations: Abraham with Hebron, Isaac with Beer-sheba and Jacob with Bethel (p. 218). This may suggest that the traditions grew up in different areas with different tribes and only later came together to form a continuous strand.

The God of the fathers

Another influential scholar, in this debate, though arguing a slightly different case, was A. Alt. Alt's interest lay in the religion of the Patriarchs. In an influential article entitled 'The God of the Fathers' ([1929] 1966, pp. 1–100), Alt noted that both the narratives in Exodus which describe Moses' call (Exod 3:13–15, normally attributed to 'E', and Exodus 6:2–3, normally attributed to 'P') refer to a change in the divine name. Exodus 3, in particular, identifies YHWH as 'the god of your fathers' (3:13). Alt became convinced that this deliberate attempt to point to continuity between the 'god of the fathers' and YHWH indicated that the religion before the time of Moses and that of Moses were originally distinct. He maintains that the 'gods of the fathers' were originally separate deities associated with different tribes. The text indicates this by the use of the titles 'the god of Abraham, the god of

Isaac and the god of Jacob'. These deities later became recognized as the one god YHWH. The passages in Exodus 3 and 6 are crucial in indicating that these pre-Mosaic deities were assimilated into Yahwistic belief.

Subsequent scholars, particularly F. M. Cross, took this debate further and investigated the names of these gods. At various places in the Hebrew Bible, both in Genesis and elsewhere, God is called by various epithets all beginning in Hebrew with the word '*el*. The most important of these are '*el 'olam* (cf. Gen 21:33, translated in the NRSV as 'the Everlasting God'), '*el 'elyon* (cf. Gen 14:18, translated as 'God Most High'), '*el ro'i* (cf. Gen 16:13, transcribed as 'El-roi'), '*el bet-el* (cf. Gen 35:7, transcribed as 'El-bethel') and '*el šadday* (cf. Gen 17:1, translated as 'God Almighty'). Alt noted the presence of these names and attributed them to local Canaanite deities. Cross, on the other hand, regarded them not as local deities but as different epithets for the god '*El*, known to have been worshipped in Canaanite and other religions (Cross's full position is set out in pp. 1–75 of *Canaanite Myth and Hebrew Epic*). These observations have led scholars to attempt to identify the nature of the religion of the Patriarchs in more detail. One recent study by A. Pagolu (1998) notes that the religion of the Patriarchs was compatible with their semi-nomadic lifestyle. The altars built by the Patriarchs were usually located outside settled communities and worship at them does not appear to have taken place in a fixed cultic setting.

This debate about patriarchal religion raises important questions about the nature of the God worshipped by Abraham, Isaac and Jacob. If the god of Abraham, Isaac and Jacob can be identified with separate local deities or with the God '*El*, this may affect the impact of the Pentateuch as a story of beginnings. In this case, the beginnings of YHWH's relationship with his people would have begun not with Abraham but with Moses. Abraham's role as the 'ancestor of faith' would be undermined. It is important to recognize, however, that the biblical account in Exodus 3 and 6 is very clear that the god who speaks to Moses is no different from the god known previously. The name used for God has changed but nothing else. The god who calls Moses *is* the god of Abraham, Isaac and Jacob. Each of the Patriarchs worshipped only one God and formed a personal relationship with this one God, who blessed and protected him. They may have had a different name for the god they worshipped but it was, nevertheless, the same god worshipped by Moses and subsequent generations of Israelites.

Questions of historicity

Form and tradition criticism speak of independent units of narrative and traditions joined together later by historical or literary events. The alert reader will have noticed that this implies a certain lack of historicity in the accounts. According to these theories, the chronology found in the text is due to later conflation or redaction, not to the actual events. Scepticism about the historicity of the patriarchal narratives is not restricted to form and tradition critics. J. Wellhausen also questioned the historicity of the narrative, suggesting that Abraham may be a 'free invention of unconscious art' (1885, p. 320). For these scholars, Abraham's actual existence as a historical figure was unimportant. Much more important was his faith and the evidence the narratives gave of Jewish belief in the relationship of God with humanity. For other scholars, the historicity of the patriarchal narratives is much more important. They cannot relegate the existence of Abraham and his descendants to the realms of unimportance. The debate was particularly fierce in the 1970s and early 1980s and gave rise to the publication of numerous studies on the subject. G. W. Ramsey's book, *The Quest for the Historical Israel* (1981), presents the arguments on both sides of the debate clearly (pp. 27–44), as well as confronting the question of the significance of the conclusions reached (pp. 107–24).

The issue is a complex one. Certain elements within the Genesis account do seem to originate from a time later than the normal dating for Abraham in the early second millennium BCE. For example, Genesis 21:34 states that Abraham 'resided as an alien many days in the land of the Philistines', but the Philistines did not settle in Canaan until around 1200 BCE, later than the time of Abraham. Another anachronism is the reference to Abraham as the father of the Arabs (25:1–5), who are only recorded as a significant force from the 800s BCE. Both T. L. Thompson (1974) and J. Van Seters (1975) remained unconvinced by the arguments in favour of the historicity of the patriarchal narratives. In detailed considerations of the evidence, they used the examples above, and many others, to demonstrate that the narratives about the Patriarchs did not originate in the second millennium BCE but much later.

Their arguments were levelled against numerous scholars who had attempted to demonstrate that various features within the Genesis stories could be traced back to the second millennium. Using archaeological evidence and evidence from the literature of other cultures from the second millennium BCE, these scholars aimed to show that the patriarchal narratives contain features that are consistent with a second millennium dating. Some arguments are more compelling than others. For example, E. A. Speiser (1967) explained the strange story of the passing off of a Patriarch's wife as his sister, which appears three times in the Genesis account (12:10–20; 20:1–18; 26:1–11), by comparing it with a Hurrian custom. This custom allowed someone to adopt his wife as his sister and thus increase her position in society and make her more secure. The value of this interpretation is that it provides a framework within which to understand an otherwise confusing narrative. Less compelling is the argument put forward by J. Bright, among others, that the personal names used in the stories, such as Terah, Abraham and Jacob, fit with those used in the Mesopotamian region of the second millennium (Bright, 1960, pp. 82–3). Thompson (1974, p. 35) pointed out that, while this is true, they also fit in the first millennium BCE. The evidence may point to a second millennium date but may also point to a later period.

In addition to attempts to show that the customs and names used in stories are consistent with a second millennium culture, there are also attempts to identify Abraham as part of a group of people known from extra-biblical sources. The best known of these is the proposal that Abraham's journey from Mesopotamia to Canaan was part of an 'Amorite infiltration' in the late third millennium – early second millennium BCE. W. F. Albright (1957, pp. 162–6) was particularly influential in associating Abraham's migration with a possible Amorite migration. The problem with the theory is that, while documentation exists for an infiltration of Semites into Mesopotamia, there is no corresponding evidence for a similar movement of Amorites into Canaan. Archaeological evidence indicates some change of culture in the period but there is little firm evidence to indicate that this change was due to an Amorite migration.

The difficulty for scholars on both sides of the argument is the lack of proof for either position. Those arguing in favour of the historicity of the narratives can only demonstrate, at best, that the stories are consistent with a second millennium dating. In other words, they can show that someone like Abraham could have existed at this time. Those arguing against historicity can only demonstrate that certain features in the narratives come from a different time period than that of Abraham. This does not prove that he did not exist, simply that the narratives may originate in a later period. The majority of the debate consists of responses to theories made by other scholars. For example, Thompson (1974), in his influential study, spent a large proportion of the work demonstrating the weakness of arguments put forward by people such as Albright. The problem is that although an argument may contain many flaws, the ability to demonstrate this does not necessarily indicate that the argument is wrong.

Genesis 12–50 in extra-biblical Jewish texts

The importance of Genesis 12–50 for later Jewish writers is ably demonstrated by the existence of numerous books based on the biblical account. The book of *Jubilees* is a retelling of the narrative of Genesis 1 to Exodus 20, which features a lengthy retelling of the Patriarchal narratives. An up-to-date translation of the text can be found in J. H. Charlesworth, *The Old Testament Pseudepigrapha* (1983, pp. 35–142). Fragments of the book were found in the excavations at Qumran and have confirmed scholars' beliefs that it was originally written in Hebrew. Its discovery at Qumran also helped to fix a date for the book, which most regard to be around 161–140 BCE. The whole book is set in the context of Moses' receiving of the law on Mount Sinai and seems to account for Moses' authorship of at least the first part of the Torah. The narrative of Genesis 1 to Exodus 20 is revealed to Moses by 'the angel of the presence', and he wrote down the account as the angel spoke. Chapters 2–10 contain a retelling of the primeval history and chapters 46–50 comprise stories about Moses. The rest of the book is occupied with a retelling and elaboration of the narratives about the Patriarchs with various parts abbreviated or omitted and additional parts added. Thus, for example, Sarah's harsh treatment of Hagar in Genesis 16:4–14 is omitted but various additional stories are included. Particularly noticeable are chapters 11–19, which tell a series of tales about Abraham's youth, and chapters 37–38, which describe a war between Jacob and Esau.

One particularly interesting feature of *Jubilees* is that Jacob becomes the focal point of the narrative, rather than Abraham as in Genesis. The book has various titles in its different versions but its most commonly used title, *Jubilees*, is taken from a reference to it in the *Damascus Document*, one of the books of community rules in the Dead Sea Scrolls: 'the book of the divisions of the times according to their jubilees and their weeks' (16:2–4). This indicates accurately the author's interest in chronology, which becomes apparent throughout the book, particularly the interest in a 364-day year which allows Jewish festivals to fall on the same day of the week each year. The reference to the book of *Jubilees* in the *Damascus Document*, and the presence of fragments of the book, demonstrate how important this reworking of the Genesis tradition was within the Qumran community. This is made even more interesting by the presence of a second retelling of Genesis among the Dead Sea Scrolls: the *Genesis Apocryphon*. Although only fragmentary, it is possible to identify that it uses a similar technique to that of the book of *Jubilees*, of retelling and embellishing the Genesis narrative.

Another embellishment of the biblical narrative, though of a different type, can be found in the story of *Joseph and Aseneth* (translation in Charlesworth, 1983, pp. 177–247). This book is thought to be a Jewish text written in Egypt between the first century BCE and the second century CE. It is an expansion of a single verse from Genesis 41:45, which records that Joseph married Aseneth, the daughter of Potiphera, priest of On. This brief statement seems to have caused considerable consternation among Jews of the time, for whom marriage outside Judaism was forbidden. This marriage was particularly problematic, as Aseneth was the daughter of an Egyptian priest. The story is a romance. Aseneth fell in love with Joseph but he would not consider her because she was a heathen. Heartbroken, Aseneth fasted for a week and at the end of the week was visited by an angel who announced that God had accepted Aseneth and had written her in the 'book of the living'. Thus it was proper for Joseph to marry his Egyptian bride.

Other collections are also based on Genesis 12–50. *The Testaments of the Three Patriarchs* consists, as its name suggests, of three 'Testaments' of Abraham, Isaac and Jacob respectively (translation in Charlesworth, 1983, pp. 774–828). Written one after another, probably between the first and third centuries CE, they are based upon the deaths of the Patriarchs and contain accounts of visits to them by an angel before they die. *The Testaments of the Twelve Patriarchs* are likewise based around the deaths of Jacob's twelve sons and purport to contain their last words to their families before death (translation in Charlesworth, 1983, pp. 869–918). They can probably be dated to the second century BCE and may have originated in Egypt. It is interesting that both collections of Testaments were adopted by Christianity and became important texts within the Eastern Church.

Abraham in the writings of Paul

Abraham was as much a figure of importance within the Christian tradition as within the Jewish tradition. For the apostle Paul, the figure of Abraham played a vital part in his argument about the relationship between Christianity and the law. In his interpretation of the narrative he uses various different techniques to support his argument of the inclusion of the Gentiles in the promises of God. In Romans 4 he concentrates on the order of the text of Genesis. He argues that, as Abraham's faith was reckoned to him as righteousness (Rom 4:3, based on Gen 15:6) before circumcision was instituted (Gen 17:24), Abraham can be regarded as the ancestor of the uncircumcised as well of the circumcised.

The argument of Galatians 3 is based upon Paul's use of various specific verses from the narrative. The crucial verses for Paul are Genesis 15:6, Genesis 18:18 (cf. also Genesis 12:3) and Genesis 12:7 (cf. also Genesis 22:17–18). Genesis 15:6 allows him to consider the significance of Abraham's faith. Genesis 18:18 and 12:7 are important for the promises they contain. Paul interprets the promise that 'all the nations of the earth shall be blessed' (18:18) as referring to the Gentiles and the words 'to your offspring' (12:7) as referring in the singular to Christ, not to the Jews. Thus these verses helped him to support his argument that the promises to Abraham were fulfilled in Christ and Christianity. Paul's use of the Hagar and Sarah story (Gal 4:21–5:1) is also interesting. His interpretation of the birth of Ishmael and Isaac is entirely allegorical. Ishmael, he maintains, stands for slavery; Isaac, for freedom. Christians are to consider themselves as Abraham's heirs according to Isaac, not according to Ishmael. There can be no doubt that the Abraham story was well-known to Paul. It was so important for him that he returned to it repeatedly in different ways in order to support his case.

The Abraham cycle (Genesis 12:1–25:18)

The Abraham cycle consists of one major theme supplemented by various additional accounts. The basic narrative focuses on the promise to Abraham to be a 'great nation'. The narrative returns to this promise repeatedly (13:14–18; 15:1–21; 17:1–27; 18:1–16a). Yet the plot of the narrative stresses the crisis that surrounds this promise: Abraham's descendants are to be blessed but he has no descendants and his wife is old and barren. The unfolding of the solution to this crisis occupies most of the Abraham cycle. The crisis continues even when Isaac is born in chapter 21, since in the following chapter Abraham is commanded by God to kill him. Interwoven with this basic plot are various sub-plots: a war between Abraham and the kings of Canaan (14); the rescue of Abraham's nephew Lot from Sodom (18:16b–19:29) and the finding of a suitable wife for Isaac (24). The deaths of, first, Sarah (23:1–20) and then Abraham (25:1–18) are also reported in the account.

Repetitions and inconsistencies in the Abraham cycle

Within the Abraham cycle, various inconsistencies and repetitions occur. For example, in Genesis 11:31–32, Terah took his family, left Ur-Kasidim, and came to Haran, where he died. In Genesis 12:1, God's command comes to Abraham to leave his land, his kindred and the house of his father. Yet, according to the narrative in Genesis 11, he had already done all of this. Another example is the account of passing one's wife off as one's sister in a situation of danger. This account is attributed twice to Abraham and Sarah (12:10–20; 20:1–18) and once to Isaac and Rebekah (26:1–11), without any reference being made to it having happened before. Source critics attribute this type of inconsistency to the accounts having originated from different sources or traditions. Thus the tradition that Abraham came from Ur is attributed to the 'P' Source and that he came from Haran to the 'J' source. The triple account of passing off a wife as a sister is attributed to oral tradition, with 12:10–20 being regarded as the base tradition and 20:1–18 and 26:1–11 as embellishments of it.

Alternative interpretations have viewed these accounts differently. D. M. Gunn and D. N. Fewell (1993) opted to read the story in its final form, rather than attempt to rediscover its origins. The picture they gain from the text of Abraham is somewhat different to the traditional portrayal of him. Abraham is renowned for his faith and ready acceptance of God's guidance. However, a close reading of the final form of the text reveals a different person. Rather than portraying a courageous, faithful figure, Gunn and Fewell propose that the text reveals 'a man of frequent surprise and great contradiction' (p. 90). When God calls to Abraham, the call

> comes at an opportune time with an opportune content: Abram is to leave his native land, which he has already done, and his father's house, of which there is nothing left, to go to the land which is already the destination of his migration. We might ask ourselves, how much faith does it take to do what one has already decided to do? (p. 91)

Gunn and Fewell suggest that the whole of the Genesis account portrays a man who acts uncertainly and at times foolishly, but who is constantly saved and protected by God. Their picture of Abraham is of a much less heroic, and much more human figure.

The account of passing off a wife as a sister has also received alternative interpretations. D. J. A Clines (1990) reads the stories not as one story embellished in three different ways but as three different stories. Through a close reading of the text, Clines was able to demonstrate that although the vehicle of the story is similar, the purpose of each one is different. In each story, the danger described is a danger to the Patriarch, not to his wife, but each narrative has a different function in its context. Genesis 12:10–20 focuses on Sarah. Immediately after the promise made to Abraham by God that he would be the father of many nations, the potential loss of Sarah becomes more crucial to the plot. The function is similar in Genesis 20 but here the danger seems cast more in the light of the potential loss of Isaac, who is born in the following chapter. The version in Genesis 26 has an entirely different function and the danger described is directed more to the Philistines, who would have suffered if they had mistreated Rebekah. This reading of the text illustrates the importance of studying each story in context, not simply as an isolated unit. Although, when considered out of context, these stories seem very similar, when considered in their context the function of each becomes much more important.

C. Exum (1999) examines these three narratives from the perspective of psychoanalysis. She claims that the story is repeated for a specific reason: there is 'a compulsive need to repeat the story until the conflict is resolved' (p. 151). She, like Clines, notes that, although scholars commonly call this story 'The Endangered Ancestress', the danger is always seen to be to the Patriarch, never to his wife. The wife remains a silent object in all versions. The reader is never given a glimpse of her opinion about the solution proposed by the Patriarch to a perceived danger to himself. In all its versions, the narrative is told from a male perspective and reveals a male fear that he will lose his beautiful wife to another, more powerful man. Exum maintains that the story reveals a conflict between 'unconscious desire that the wife gain sexual knowledge of another man and the fear that this could happen' (p. 151). It is only in the final rendering of the story (chapter 26) that the conflict is resolved. Despite having been in the land for a long time (v. 8), no one had taken Isaac's wife. The moral code of the Philistines is revealed through Abimelech's horror at discovering that Rebekah is Isaac's wife. According to Exum, at this point the fantasy is abandoned and the conflict resolved.

The promises to Abraham

The promises to the Patriarchs are the focal points of the narrative in Genesis 12–50. So much so, that Clines (1997) suggests that they are the key for understanding the whole of the Pentateuch. The promise in 12:1–2, that begins Genesis 12–50, contains three themes which Clines maintains are drawn out in the rest of the Pentateuch.

> Now the Lord said to Abram, 'Go from your country and your kindred and your father's house to the land that I will show you. I will make of you a great nation, and I will bless you, and make your name great, so that you will be a blessing.' (Gen 12:1–2)

These three themes are the promise of descendants ('I will make of you a great nation'); the promise of relationship with God ('I will bless you, and make your name great') and the promise of land ('Go from your country ... to the land that I will show you'). As well as being present throughout the Pentateuch, these promises are woven firmly into the fabric of the Abraham story itself. The whole narrative portrays the slow unfolding of Abraham's relationship with God. The crises that surround the production of an heir and is played out on the canvas of Abraham's new dwelling in the land of Canaan.

Although these promises appear throughout the Abraham cycle, they reach a particular climax in the double account of the making of a covenant between God and Abraham in chapters 15 and 17. Scholars consider the covenant, described in chapter 15, to come from the 'J' Source with possible additions from the 'E' source. Some, such as Wellhausen, regard verses 1–6 as 'E'; others, such as Gunkel, see 'E' interwoven throughout the whole narrative (vv. 1b, 3a, 5, 11, 12a, 13a, 14, 16); and others again think that 'E' does not feature at all (see the discussion in Wenham, 1987, p. 326). Whatever its origins the passage falls into two distinct sections: God's promise of descendants with Abraham's acceptance of this promise (vv. 1–6) and the ritual of the ratification of the covenant (vv. 7–21). Wenham observes (p. 325) that these two sections are roughly parallel with each other, beginning with a promise and ending with ratification of the promise, first through Abraham's faith and second through YHWH's covenant.

One of the most striking elements of this covenant is the strange ritual of ratification described in verses 9–18. Here Abraham is commanded to cut in two a calf, a goat, a ram, a dove and a turtle dove. After dark, a smoking pot and a flaming torch are passed through the middle of the animals. The significance of this action is not entirely clear. Verse 18 states that God 'cut a covenant' (NRSV translates the phrase 'made a covenant') with Abraham on that day. Thus, this action seems to provide the proof requested by Abraham (v. 8) that the promise would be fulfilled. This ceremony does seem to explain the use of the term in Hebrew to 'cut a covenant', used in the Hebrew Bible to describe the making of a covenant. Jeremiah 34:18 describes a similar practice of passing between the parts of a calf as the enactment of a curse. Wenham (1987) regards this as suggesting that YHWH's action invokes a curse on himself if he does not keep the promise made to Abraham.

The covenant in chapter 17, examined in the previous chapter in the context of the importance of the theme of covenant for the Priestly Writer, places an obligation, not on God, but on Abraham. In this account, the sign of the covenant is to take place regularly: the circumcision of every male member of the household. Again, the promise of the covenant is of descendants, relationship and land. One of the most striking elements of this account is the change of name from Abram to Abraham. The name 'Abram', meaning in Hebrew 'the father of exaltation', is exchanged for 'Abraham', which has no apparent meaning in Hebrew. The most obvious reason for its inclusion is a play on words, since the word *hamon* (translated 'multitude' in the NRSV) begins with the letters added into Abram to make it Abraham.

Sarah and Isaac; Hagar and Ishmael

The account of the crisis surrounding the birth of a possible heir for Abraham is focused on Sarah's ability to bear children. This theme occupies a large portion of the Abraham cycle. Although the crucial need for heirs is Abraham's, the shame for barrenness is Sarah's. The narrative stresses the impossibility of the situation by indicating that, in addition to being infertile, Sarah is 90. Tension is established in the story between God's promise and the apparent impossibility of its fulfilment. Although this collection of stories is known as the Abraham cycle, the character of Sarah is central to the account. In many places in the narrative she acts as silent foil to the male hero Abraham. Although present, she is often portrayed as irrelevant to the main narrative. Thus we do not know her opinion on the command to leave her home in Mesopotamia and journey to a new land, nor what she thought of God's command to Abraham in Genesis 22 to kill her only son. However, in certain places, Sarah's voice is heard within the narrative. Perhaps the most important example of this is her interaction with Hagar, the Egyptian slave girl who at Sarah's behest bore a son to Abraham. Unsurprisingly, this sub-narrative has become the focus for many feminist interpretations of the text.

Sarah and Hagar's relationship is one of power and oppression. The powerful wife, Sarah, has need of the powerless slave, Hagar, and yet feels threatened by the shifting patterns of power when Hagar produces a son, the one thing Sarah cannot have. The relationship between Sarah and Hagar is set out primarily in two passages: Genesis 16:1–16 and 21:8–21. Source critics identify these narratives as originating from two sources, 'J' and 'E' respectively. However, although these stories do present a similar theme of the banishment of Hagar by Sarah, it is easier to see them as following one from the other than as overlapping. In the first narrative, Hagar flees Sarah's cruel treatment while pregnant but is persuaded by an angel to return; in the second, she is evicted by Sarah and finds a new life with her son in Egypt. Both stories tell of God's increasing protection of Hagar as her situation worsens. This portrayal of power and oppression makes these stories of rival women even more interesting.

Sarah is often portrayed as the heroine in this story, and yet her treatment of Hagar is oppressive and violent. The eviction of a slave into the desert would have been tantamount to murder, had not God protected Hagar and Ishmael. D. N. Fewell (1998) reflects further on this dynamic of power in her retelling of the story from Hagar's perspective. She focuses on the meaning of Ishmael's name, 'God hears', to draw out the theme of divine protection for Hagar. P. S. Kramer (1998) explores the theme of pairs of women in more detail. She notes that within the patriarchal stories women are more often portrayed as rivals than as friends; Sarah and Hagar are a good example of this. While both Fewell and Kramer are interested in the literary form of the narrative, S. J. Teubal (1993) attempts to understand the text from a historical viewpoint. She maintains that the clash between Sarah and Hagar should be understood from the perspective of Mesopotamian culture. She argues that Sarah was a Matriarch in her own right and that Sarah, Rebekah and Rachel were all Mesopotamian priestesses. Section 146 of the code of Hammurabi indicates that the practice of a handmaid bearing a child for a priestess was well known within Mesopotamian culture (p. 236). However, Hagar was not Mesopotamian but Egyptian. The conflict that arose between the two women stems from a cultural misunderstanding, in that the Egyptian Hagar attempted to introduce customs unacceptable to the Mesopotamian Sarah.

Abraham and Lot

The presence of Lot in the Abraham cycle appears at first glance to be an unimportant subplot in the main account of God's promise to Abraham. W. Brueggemann (1982, pp. 95–6) has pointed out, however, that Lot's presence in the account functions to emphasize Abraham's lack of an heir. Alongside the presence of Ishmael, the illegitimate son of Abraham, Abraham's nephew, Lot seems to emphasize the frustration of Abraham's position. He has two 'almost but not quite' heirs. What he needs is one genuine one. L. A. Turner (1990) considers the character of Lot as portrayed in the Genesis account. He maintains that Lot comes over as a complex figure who exhibits the traits of both wickedness and righteousness in the same narrative.

L. M. Bechtel (1998) turns her attention to Genesis 19, the account that ends with the destruction of Sodom because of its wickedness. This narrative completes a section which seems to reflect on hospitality, beginning in Genesis 18:1–9 (though Genesis 21:1–7, the birth of Isaac, also refers back to this section). The account features three messengers who are later revealed by the text to be the Lord (18:22) and two angels (19:1). The account seems to reflect a common theme within mythology of the importance of welcoming strangers. Von Rad ([1956] 1972, p. 205) draws a parallel with the Greek story of the three gods, Zeus, Poseidon and Hermes, who visit Hyrieus in Boeotia. Hyrieus' hospitality is rewarded by the gift of a longed-for son, as is Abraham's hospitality here. The narrative continues in 18:22 as the two angels go on their way to destroy Sodom and Abraham pleads for its salvation. In her reading of Genesis 19:1–11, Bechtel criticizes traditional interpretations of the passage for understanding the narrative from the modern Western world's perspective, not from the perspective of biblical society. She maintains that most interpretations, which view the sin of Sodom as being the practice of homosexuality, are based upon a perspective oriented towards the individual. A more group-oriented reading of the text indicates that the narrative is not concerned with sexuality but with xenophobia. The sin of the people of Sodom was to exclude outsiders from their community. Bechtel argues that this narrative stresses the importance of inclusion and openness within the society of early Israel.

Abraham and Isaac

The birth of Isaac represents the climax of the whole Abraham cycle. The promises made to Abraham throughout this section are dependent upon Isaac's birth and subsequent survival. Isaac's long awaited birth occurs in chapter 21, and yet this climax of the narrative is subtly undermined both in this chapter and the next. Chapter 21 also tells of the banishment of Hagar by Sarah and the near death of Ishmael, Hagar's son. The birth of Isaac almost causes the death of Abraham's other son, Ishmael. God's promise that Abraham will be the ancestor of many nations hangs in the balance once more. Even more surprising are the events of chapter 22, where, the narrative describes God's command to Abraham to sacrifice Isaac. The future of Abraham's long-promised heir is by no means certain. As R. W. L. Moberly (1992) observes: 'Israel's very existence hung, apparently, by a thread'(p. 50).

This narrative became significant within Jewish exegesis. Rabbinic interpretations of the story of Genesis 22:1–19 are known as the '*aqedah* (binding) or '*aqedah Yishaq* (the binding of Isaac). P. S. Alexander (1990) has reviewed the major features of this exegesis in his article on the '*aqedah in A Dictionary of Biblical Interpretation*. Within rabbinic exegesis, the story of the binding of Isaac was a complex collection of ideas, covering numerous aspects of the narrative. When referring to the story, the Rabbis based their discussion not only on the biblical version of the story but also on the traditions that had grown up around it within Judaism. Alexander has identified the three most important elements contained within these traditions. The first element found in Jewish tradition is that Isaac was a willing victim of the proposed sacrifice. The Targum *Pseudo-Jonathan* states that Isaac was not a young boy at the time of the sacrifice but 37 years old. The decision to sacrifice him arose out of an argument between himself and Ishmael about who would give the greatest sacrifice to God – Isaac offered his whole body.

A second common element found in these traditions is that the sacrifice took place on the site of the temple in Jerusalem. Consequently, the sacrifice of Isaac acts as the ideal type for all subsequent sacrifices. Subsequent sacrifices are efficacious because they recall the *'aqedah*. The final most common element within these traditions is the belief that the *'aqedah* acted in some way for the benefit of Isaac's descendants. Alexander observes that this part of the tradition takes two forms. The first is that the obedience of Abraham and Isaac 'were works of supererogation which laid up merit for their descendants' (p. 45); the second that Isaac acted as a representative for his descendants. Thus, his action atoned for the sins of those that came after him. This final element of the traditions bears a remarkable resemblance to the Christian doctrine of the atonement. The parallels noted between these two have raised questions of a connection between them. While it is possible that the Jewish *'aqedah* tradition influenced the Christian tradition of the atoning sacrifice of Christ or vice versa, Alexander sees no reason to suppose a direct connection between the two. Instead, he argues that it is conceivable that the two traditions could have grown up independently of each other and that this is more likely than a direct borrowing of one from the other.

Despite the importance of the birth and survival of Isaac for the patriarchal narrative, his character remains remarkably undeveloped. With a few exceptions (e.g. Gen 24), the focus of the narrative passes straight from Abraham to Isaac's two sons, Jacob and Esau. Isaac is portrayed as a shadowy figure, significant primarily for his continuance of Abraham's line. In an article published in 1990, C. Exum and J. W. Whedbee reflected upon the elusiveness of his character and the significance of his name. The name Isaac means, in Hebrew, 'he laughs'. Yet Isaac is only portrayed as a joyful figure at his birth. Sarah's cynical laughter of 18:12, when she heard God's promise of a child, turned to laughter of joy at his birth: 'Sarah said, "God has brought laughter for me; everyone who hears will laugh with me"' (21:6). For the most part, in the rest of the narrative Isaac is portrayed as a 'victim through and through, characteristically acquiescent to personages stronger and more clever than he' (Exum and Whedbee, 1990, p. 130). Even in the passages in which Isaac features, his role is a passive one. In her article, L. Teugels (1994) examines the relationship between Isaac and Rebekah in Genesis 24 and elsewhere. She notes that it is Rebekah who is the strong character, not Isaac, as one would expect from other portrayals of women in the patriarchal narrative. Isaac is the passive bearer of the promise of God, whereas Rebekah is the active character who ensures that the promise is passed on to her favourite son, Jacob.

The Jacob cycle (Genesis 25:19–35:29)

In contrast to Isaac, the character of Jacob is well defined in the biblical narrative. Even his name fits his character better than that of Isaac. The biblical narrative gives two etymologies for the name Jacob. Genesis 25:26 ties the name to the Hebrew word 'aqeb, which means heel, whereas Genesis 27:36 associates it with 'aqab, meaning cheat. Both these etymologies of the name give the impression of an active character who is determined to achieve his aims by any means possible. Such is the character of Jacob in the biblical narrative. In Genesis 32:29 and 35:10 he is renamed Israel. The whole narrative circles around his bearing of the promise of God, achieved by tricking his elder brother Esau out of his birthright. The tensions which surround God's promise still form the focus of the narrative. This time the crisis is not concerned with continuity but with the land. Jacob tricks the birthright from his brother and is driven from the land. As a result, the question which hangs over the whole of the Jacob narrative is whether God's promise can be fulfilled outside the land. It is only with Jacob's return in Genesis 32 that the crisis is resolved once more.

R. Alter (1981, pp. 42–6) draws out some of the complexities of the conflict between Jacob and Esau. The text of Genesis 25:23 identifies Jacob and Esau as 'the eponymous founders of two neighbouring and rival peoples' (p. 42). If the narrative is read in this way, the descriptions of Esau as red and hairy-skinned (25:25), with a large appetite (25:29–34), associate him with primal, almost beast-like qualities. Such a portrayal legitimates the less than human treatment of Esau's descendants – the Edomites – by Jacob's descendants – the Israelites. In fact, there is even more to the story than this. Although Esau is portrayed as unthinking and impetuous, Jacob is revealed as an ambiguous character, mercenary and scheming. His fitness to bear the promise to Abraham seems to be based not simply on personal quality but on the double theophany he receives in Genesis 28 and 32. Despite his personality, the revelation of God to him makes him fit to be the bearer of God's promise. Alter points out (p. 45) that there is a certain 'symmetrical poetic justice' in the fact that Jacob himself is tricked as he tricked his father and brother. Jacob took advantage of his father's bad eyesight to cheat Esau out of his birthright; Laban used the bridal veil to trick Jacob into marrying Leah instead of Rachel.

The characters of Rachel and Leah are not as well defined as that of Rebekah. They have become simply the bargaining chips in the power struggle between Laban and Jacob. Where Rebekah is shown to be an active, thinking subject, Rachel and Leah, on the whole, play a much more passive role in the story. However, J. E. Lapsley (1998) has attempted to understand more about Rachel in the context of the Genesis narrative. She focuses her attention on Rachel's response to her father in Genesis 31:35: 'Let not my lord be angry that I cannot rise before you, for the way of women is upon me'. This response allowed Rachel to deceive her father and steal the household gods for which he was searching. Lapsley regards this as the faintest hint of a female voice within a male narrative. She maintains that, while the words are a lie, they convey truth in that they represent the inequity of Rachel's position in patriarchal society and constitute a resistance and protest to this position.

Another woman featured in the Jacob cycle is Dinah, Jacob's daughter (Gen 34). This narrative does not appear to fit easily into the flow of the Jacob cycle and is more concerned with the action of Dinah's brothers than that of her father. The narrative tells of the rape of Dinah by Shechem, the son of a city chief, and the vengeance wreaked upon the city by Dinah's brothers. Traditional interpretations of this passage understand it in similar terms to the author of the text: as an act of 'burning shame done to the brothers' (von Rad, [1956] 1972, p. 334). S. Scholz (1998), however, directs her attention to the feature in the text, generally accepted by scholars, that Shechem attempted to woo Dinah after raping her. This is often regarded as mitigation for the act of rape which precedes it. By means of a detailed consideration of the verbs used in the text, Scholz maintains the importance of recognizing that this account is not a love story but is a story that recounts sexual violence.

The Joseph narrative (Genesis 37–50)

The final section of Genesis turns its attention to the life of one of Jacob's twelve sons, Joseph. Joseph was the eleventh son of Jacob and the first son of Jacob's favourite wife, Rachel. Although a part of the patriarchal narrative, the Joseph narrative stands out as unusual. The Abraham and Jacob cycles consist of small units loosely bound together to form a chronological history. The Joseph narrative seems to be a much more complete narrative, with a clear plot and progression from one section to another. For this reason, it is common to refer to Genesis 37–50 as the Joseph narrative, not the Joseph cycle (as in the Abraham and Jacob cycles). The chapters seem to form a novella with a clear beginning and end and development of character throughout. The overall narrative tells of the success of Joseph in the face of familial conflict. Joseph, the favourite son of his father, alienates his brothers, who send him into slavery (37). Various factors lead to success in the Egyptian court and a position of great authority (41:46–57). A severe famine drives his family to beg for aid in Egypt. Joseph provides the help that they need and becomes united with his family once more (42–50). Interwoven with this basic narrative are two other narratives: the account of Judah and Tamar and the cycle of stories about Joseph's time in Egypt. Although this latter cycle of stories accounts for Joseph's rise to success in the Egyptian court, upon which the main narrative depends, chapters 39–41 seem to be a coherent whole in their own right.

The apparent unity of the text is one of the striking features of this account. This has led certain source critics to propose that the Joseph narrative was a complete, originally independent, text, inserted as a whole into the Genesis narrative. For example, C. Westermann (1988, pp. 257–8) regards the account as a 'single, self-contained document' dating to the period of the early monarchy. He does not, however, consider the author to be 'J', on the grounds that the style and theology of the account differ significantly from the writings of 'J' found elsewhere in Genesis. Whatever the identity of the author, the person responsible for the writing of this account seems to be accustomed to Egyptian life and customs. Life in the Egyptian court, including the existence of court officials and counsellors, is accurately portrayed in the narrative. The account of Joseph and Potiphar's wife in chapter 39 finds an interesting parallel in Egyptian literature. The Egyptian account of the Two Brothers (*ANET*, 23–5) tells of a younger brother who worked for his elder brother. One day, the wife of the elder brother attempted to persuade the younger brother to sleep with her. When he refused, the elder brother's wife accused him falsely to her husband. This account bears obvious parallels to the Joseph story, though it does not necessarily indicate that the author of the Joseph narrative copied it.

R. Alter (1981, pp. 159–76) has observed that the whole Joseph narrative revolves around knowledge. The hero, Joseph, has divinely inspired knowledge, given through dreams, which allows him to foresee what will happen to his brothers (they will bow down and worship him, 37:5–11), to his fellow prisoners (the cup-bearer will be freed and the baker executed, 40:1–19) and to Egypt (it will have seven years of plenty followed by seven years of famine, 41:25–36). Alongside this are the counter-figures who do not have knowledge: Pharaoh (who does not know the meaning of his dream, 41:1–8) and Joseph's brothers (who do not know Joseph when they meet him again, 42:8). Alter maintains that this theme is one which makes the Joseph narrative such a compelling story.

Concluding remarks

The magisterial account of Abraham and his descendants began in the territory of one major empire in the ancient Near East, Mesopotamia, and ends in another, Egypt. In the course of Genesis 12–50, the tension which surrounded God's original promise to Abraham of descendants, a relationship with God and the gift of land, has arisen, been resolved and has arisen once more. The first crisis surrounded the birth of an heir to Abraham, the second and third concerned the exile of the bearer of the promise from Canaan. First Jacob was banished, due to his quarrel with Esau, and then Joseph was sold into slavery in Egypt. Despite the extended account of God's intervention to save Joseph, given in Genesis 37–50, the crisis is merely postponed, not resolved. Indeed, the account ends with Jacob and his whole family living in Egypt, away from the land promised to them by God. The scene is set, therefore, for the next stage in the account of the beginnings of Israel, a stage in which Abraham's descendants once more come near to the land promised to them by God.

5

Let my people go ...

Exodus 1–15: Liberation from slavery

The book of Exodus begins where Genesis ends: in Egypt. It acts as a sequel to the events described in the Joseph narrative. Exodus 1:8 in particular ('now a new king arose over Egypt, who did not know Joseph') seems to indicate that we are to understand what follows as the next episode in the story. Almost as soon as it begins, however, it becomes clear that the nature of the account has changed. The story no longer describes a family history, with a single significant 'Patriarch' as leader. Joseph's descendants are now 'numerous' and 'powerful' (Exod 1:9). While they cannot yet be regarded as a 'nation', they are no longer simply a family grouping. The altered nature of the people also leads to a different kind of leader. Moses is chosen by God to lead the people, not by virtue of rank or birthright, but by virtue of divine calling. Although Exodus clearly follows on from the Genesis narrative, the situation is very different. As Genesis 12–50 moved the story of beginnings on from a universal history to the history of a chosen family of God, so Exodus also moves the story on from a family history towards the history of the people of God.

The book of Exodus falls easily into four sections. Exodus 1:1–12:36 describes the situation of the people in Egypt; Exodus 12:37–15:21 recounts the exodus from Egypt; Exodus 15:22–18:27 describes the wandering in the wilderness; and Exodus 19:1–40:30 narrates the giving of the law to Moses on Sinai. The first two sections explore the theme of this current chapter: exodus and liberation. The latter two sections of Exodus present the themes of wilderness wanderings and law also found in the remaining books of the Pentateuch (Leviticus, Numbers and Deuteronomy). For this reason, Exodus 15:22–40:30 will be explored in more detail in Chapters 6 and 7. The concern of this chapter is the account and significance of the liberation of the people of God in the exodus event.

The event of the exodus is one of the defining moments within the history of the people of God. God's action in the exodus was significant not only at the time, but also for all subsequent generations of Israelites. It is cited repeatedly throughout the Hebrew Bible as evidence of God's intervention within history. Assurance that God does and will act is based upon the exodus event. In addition to its importance within the literature of the Hebrew Bible, the exodus was also central to the cultic life of Israel. Three of the major festivals (Passover, the feast of the unleavened bread and the feast of the firstlings) are all connected, in some way, with the events of the exodus. Its cultic significance ensured that the exodus was not simply a historical event but that it also had continuous contemporary significance within the life of faith. The exodus functions as a central event within the life of Israel, important both as a defining moment in history and celebrated throughout subsequent generations for its lasting significance.

History and the exodus tradition

The nature of the exodus account raises questions about when and where it happened. The biblical text provides certain information, such as the names of cities or other places, that indicate that it should be possible to date the events described and work out the location of the places mentioned. Attempts to do this use evidence both from within the text and from extra-biblical Near Eastern texts. Names and dates from key verses and passages can be compared with evidence from archaeology and other texts to fix the account within a historical context. One of the problems with this attempt, however, is that in many cases the event can be associated with more than one date or more than one location. Choosing which is the correct date and location can often be fraught with difficulties.

When did the exodus happen?

One of the problems for dating the exodus is that it is not something that can be done in isolation. The date of the exodus is integrally linked to the date of the settlement of the people in Canaan, the account of which is recorded in the books of Joshua and Judges. The biblical account places the exodus approximately 40 years before the people settled in the land of Canaan. Consequently, the date proposed for the settlement clearly affects the date proposed for the exodus. However, the events of the settlement are outside the remit of the present study and have been well explored elsewhere (see particularly Mills, 1999, pp. 13–33). Therefore, what follows is a consideration of the factors that affect the dating of the exodus only, although a final judgement on dating cannot be made without a similar consideration of the factors that affect the dating of the settlement.

Two major periods have been proposed for the date of the exodus: the fifteenth century BCE and the thirteenth century BCE. A fifteenth-century date for the exodus is suggested by 1 Kings 6:1: 'In the four hundred and eightieth year after the Israelites came out of the land of Egypt, in the fourth year of Solomon's reign over Israel, in the month of Ziv, which is the second month, he began to build the house of the Lord.' The fourth year of Solomon's reign is commonly dated to around 966 BCE. This would place the exodus 480 years earlier, in 1446 BCE. For many years, this date was commonly accepted as correct and has also been supported more recently by J. J. Bimson (1978). There are, however, numerous problems with a fifteenth-century date for the exodus and settlement. One of these is that, if the generations between the exodus and the fourth year of Solomon's reign are combined, the number of years reached is over 553 years, not 480. This raises questions about how the ancient biblical writers calculated dates and generations.

Problems such as this caused scholars such as H. H. Rowley (1950) to abandon a fifteenth century date in favour of a date in the thirteenth century. Evidence which suggests the thirteenth century includes the reference in Exodus 1:11 to the building of the store cities Pithom and Rameses by the Israelites in Egypt. Rameses II was king in Egypt from 1304–1237 BCE and the city Pi-Ramesse was built during his reign and named after him. The city of Rameses mentioned in Exodus 1:11 may well be this city, Pi-Ramesse. This date is further supported by the Merneptah Stele. Merneptah, the son of Rameses II, ruled in Egypt between 1212 and 1202 BCE. Archaeologists have found a stele, a large standing block of stone, engraved with a record of his many victories. One of these victories was a subjugation of Israel in Canaan, which suggests that by the time of Merneptah the Israelites had already settled in Israel. A discussion of the different theories suggesting a date in the fifteenth century, thirteenth century or combination of the two, including a consideration of the relevant evidence for the dating of the settlement, can be found in W. Johnstone (1990), pp. 20–6.

Who were the people mentioned in the exodus account?

Two questions arise in a consideration of the people mentioned in the exodus narrative. The first concerns the number of people who left Egypt. Exodus 12:37 states that the number of people who left in the exodus were 600,000 men plus women and children. W. Johnstone

(1990) estimates that if most of the men were married, then the total number of leavers would be around 2 or 3 million. This causes some problems with the biblical account. It would be impossible for so many people to cross a stretch of water in the space of a night or to be able to survive in the desert for forty years. Johnstone points out that modern census figures indicate that the total current Bedouin population in the Sinai peninsula is 40,000 (pp. 27–8). Johnstone suggests two solutions to this problem. Either the Hebrew *'eleph* should be taken to mean family (rather than a thousand), as it is in Judges 6:15 and 1 Samuel 10:19; or the number 600,000, like other statistics in the Hebrew Bible, is not accurate. Another more radical solution to the question of how many people left Egypt is that it was only a few tribes not the whole of the Israelite nation. J. Wellhausen (1885), while accepting the basic veracity of the exodus tradition, proposed that those entering and subsequently leaving Egypt were a small group of tribal herdsmen. H. H. Rowley (1950, pp. 116–23) maintained that those who left were members of the Joseph tribes (Ephraim and Manasseh), while J. Bright (1960) maintains they were a 'mixed group, by no means all descendants of Jacob' (p. 121), who later spread their exodus tradition to all the Israelites.

Other attempts to identify the characters involved in the exodus try to associate those mentioned with groups known from extra-biblical sources. Two of these groups of people are the Hyksos and the Habiru (also known as the Hapiru, 'Apiru or Khapiru). The Hyksos were the rulers of Egypt in the 'second intermediate period' (roughly 1786–1529 BCE). Records indicate that they invaded Egypt and were probably of Semitic origin. The Jewish historian Josephus, who claimed to have taken his information from an Egyptian historian, Manetho, associated Joseph's arrival in Egypt with that of the Hyksos. If the tradition in Genesis 15:13 that the people were in Egypt for four hundred years is correct *and* if a thirteenth-century date is accepted for the exodus, then Joseph's arrival in Egypt would correspond with that of the Hyksos. This would certainly explain why the Semitic Joseph was so successful in an alien culture. While this theory is attractive, other biblical verses suggest that the sojourn in Egypt was much shorter, only four generations (Gen 15:16; Exod 6:16–20). This makes a connection with the Hyksos less likely.

The Habiru are a group of people referred to in numerous sources from the second millennium BCE, most notably in one of the Amarna letters from a Jerusalemite chieftain to Egypt in 1375 BCE. This band of people were an invading force who troubled many different regions around this period. The similarity between the name Habiru and 'Hebrew' inevitably led scholars to propose a connection between the two groups. Indeed, if there was a connection between them, this would further support a fifteenth-century date for the exodus. A detailed consideration of the texts referring to Habiru, however, indicates that the term was not an ethnic one but a social one. It referred to groups of people who lived on the outskirts of society. They were normally foreigners who had left their own countries in an attempt to forge a living elsewhere. Their presence seems to have been a general phenomenon of the Late Bronze Age period. Consequently, while the Israelite might have been identified as Habiru, it would be hard to prove that the Habiru referred to in the Amarna letters were in fact the Israelites. While the connections proposed between the biblical narrative, the Hyksos and the Habiru are alluring, there is insufficient evidence to support the view with certainty.

The location of the Red Sea

Another historical question raised by the text is the location of the sea crossed by Moses and the people as they left Egypt. The English phrase 'Red Sea' (cf. Exod 15:22) translates the phrases used in the Vulgate and Septuagint, both of which mean 'Red Sea' and are used elsewhere to refer to the north-west section of the Indian Ocean which separates Africa from Arabia. The northernmost sections of the sea split into two gulfs: the Gulf of Suez, which runs between the Sinai desert and Egypt and the Gulf of Aqabah, which runs between the Sinai desert and the desert of Arabia. The 'Red Sea' can refer to either one of these gulfs or to the main section of the sea. The slight complexity is that the Hebrew *yam suph* means literally 'sea of reeds'. This has led to considerable debate about its location. The question facing scholars is whether the phrase 'sea of reeds' refers to a description of what the sea was like or whether it was the name of the sea. There is little consensus on the issue. Some point to the presence of a marshy area along the route of the modern Suez canal as a possible location for the 'sea of reeds'. Others note that 1 Kings 9:26 refers to the Gulf of Aqabah as the 'sea of reeds', suggesting that the traditional 'Red Sea' might be an appropriate description here.

Exodus and Sinai

In the book of Exodus, the giving of the law on Sinai and the exit from Egypt have equal importance. The first half of the book contains a description of leaving Egypt (Exod 1–18); the second half (19–40) contains an account of the giving of the law to Moses on Sinai. The one is firmly accompanied by the other. As a part of the story of beginnings,

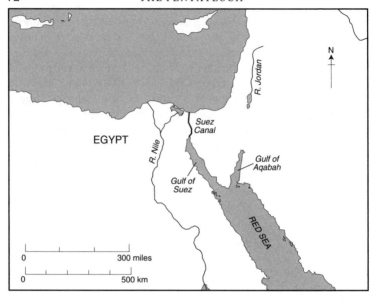

Map 3: Possible locations of the 'Red Sea'

the leaving of Egypt and the giving of the law on Sinai are linked. God's action of liberation in leading the people out of Egypt is one side of the covenant made with the people. The people's side of the covenant is to obey the requirements laid upon them in the law given at Sinai. Exodus and Sinai form two sides of the same covenantal coin: the former establishes God's responsibility; the latter sets out the people's responsibility.

However, a detailed examination of the text of the book of Exodus led Wellhausen (1885) to note that, particularly within the 'J' account, the accounts of exodus and Sinai are not seamlessly linked. Wellhausen noted particularly the tradition recorded in Exodus 15–18, associated with Kadesh, which referred to YHWH making for the people 'a statute and an ordinance'. Furthermore, this collection of narratives based at Kadesh continues in Numbers 10–14. He maintained that this indicates that the original exodus narrative was connected with a giving of the law in Kadesh. The Sinai account (Exod 19–24 and 32–34), he maintained, was originally separate and inserted later. G. von Rad ([1938] 1966) drew on this theory to support his own proposal that the events of the exodus and Sinai were originally separate. He directed his attention to numerous passages that retold the account of the exodus, the most important being Deuteronomy 26:5b–9 (two others were Deut 6:21–23 and Josh 24:2–13):

'A wandering Aramean was my ancestor; he went down into Egypt and lived there as an alien, few in number, and there he became a great nation, mighty and populous. When the Egyptians treated us harshly and afflicted us, by imposing hard labour on us, we cried to the Lord, the God of our ancestors; the Lord heard our voice and saw our affliction, our toil, and our oppression. The Lord brought us out of Egypt with a mighty hand and an outstretched arm, with a terrifying display of power, and with signs and wonders; and he brought us into this place and gave us this land, a land flowing with milk and honey.'

This passage records the words that the Israelites were commanded to say when they brought an offering at the festival of the first-fruits. Using a form-critical approach, von Rad identified it as an ancient credal statement which had been incorporated into the text. He noted that while the exodus plays a central role in the text, Sinai is not mentioned at all. Consequently, he argued that these two accounts were not originally connected and were only connected later by the creative genius of the writer of the 'J' source. M. Noth ([1954] 1960, pp. 127–38) also argued that exodus and Sinai were originally separate. He maintained that it was possible to identify five major themes in the early history of Israel: the promise to the Patriarchs; the exodus from Egypt; the wandering in the wilderness; the revelation at Sinai; and the settlement. These five themes, he argued, were originally separate traditions which were joined later, not by the 'J' writer as von Rad proposed, but in the amphictyony.

This view has been widely challenged by scholars. E. W. Nicholson (1973) surveyed the major arguments on both sides. Although there are many objections to the separation of the exodus traditions from the Sinai traditions, two crucial ones stand out. The first concerns the nature of the so-called 'credal statements'; the second considers the importance of the covenant. Von Rad's proposal that the credal statements which he identified in Deuteronomy and Joshua indicate that the exodus tradition was originally separate from the Sinai tradition, is based on the assumption that these so-called credal statements were ancient expressions of belief. More recent scholarship has questioned this assumption. N. Lohfink (1994) has argued that there was an ancient centre to the credal statement in Deuteronomy 26, which he identified as

A wandering Aramean was my ancestor –
but see, now I bring the first of the fruit of the ground that you,
YHWH, have given me! (p. 283)

but that the rest is a later Deuteronomic expansion. This means that the bulk of this passage cannot be taken as evidence for ancient belief about anything. Another even more significant question is whether confessions of faith are a genuine part of Israelite religion or an import from Christian scholarship. The concept of a confession of faith, while being an essential element of Christian belief, sits uncomfortably with Israelite religion (see Nicholson, 1973, p. 25).

A second problem with the separation of the exodus and Sinai traditions, as proposed by von Rad, is that it makes the concept of covenant a late development in the history of Israel. The centrality of the concept of covenant to Israelite faith makes this unlikely. G. E. Mendenhall has argued in many places, most recently in his article with G. A. Herion on 'Covenant' in *The Anchor Bible Dictionary* (1992, pp. 1179–202), that the concept of covenant can be demonstrated to be ancient. One of the major grounds for his argument is a comparison between the Sinai covenant and Hittite treaties of the Bronze Age period. Treaties were common in the ancient Near Eastern world and existed in various forms. Those which caught the attention of Mendenhall came from the Hittites between 1460 and 1215 BCE. The Hittite Empire was roughly located in the region of Anatolia and northern Syria. The rulers of this empire established relationships with the peoples they conquered (their vassals) by means of a treaty, which laid out the obligations of the people to their overlords (the suzerain).

Mendenhall maintains that it is possible to identify similarities between the Sinai covenant and these Hittite treaties. In particular he noted seven characteristics, laid out below, which both the Hittite treaties and the Sinai covenant share. He maintained that the overlap between these two indicates that the Sinai covenant was modelled on the earlier Hittite treaties and, consequently, can be demonstrated to be ancient.

Table 6: Parallels between Hittite treaties and the Sinai covenant

Element of treaty	Form in Hittite treaty	Biblical parallels identified by Mendenhall
(1) Identification of covenant giver	Begins 'The Words of ...' and gives name, titles and genealogy of king,	'I am the Lord your God, who brought you out of the land of Egypt ...' Exod 20:2
(2) Historical prologue	The Hittite king recounts the deeds which have benefitted the vassal	As (1) above

Table 6: Continued

Element of treaty	Form in Hittite treaty	Biblical parallels identified by Mendenhall
(3) Treaty stipulations	Describes the vassals' obligations	The Ten Commandments (Exod 20:3–17)
(4) Provision to deposit treaty in temple	Sets out that the treaty should be deposited in the vassals' temple and read out regularly	Tablets deposited in the ark of the covenant (e.g. Exod 25:21)
(5) List of witnesses to treaty	Lengthy lists of deities who acted as witnesses to the treaty	E.g. 'Give ear, O heavens, and I will speak ...' Deut 32:1
(6) Curses and blessings formulae	List of the consequences of obedience and disobedience	See for example Deut 28
(7) The ratification ceremony	The formal ritual which brought the treaty into being	Sacrifice, e.g. Exod 24:5–8

Furthermore, Mendenhall maintains that the covenant had the vital sociological function of holding the Israelites together as a group before the period of the early monarchy. For him, the separation of the covenant at Sinai from the exodus tradition would undermine this important function.

Although Mendenhall's theory has been influential in arguing for an early date for the concept of covenant in the history of Israel, there are a number of problems with his theory, many of which have been pointed out by D. J. McCarthy (1963, pp. 152–67). Perhaps the most important of these is that, although Mendenhall is able to demonstrate that all the major features of a Hittite treaty can be found in the biblical account, they are not all found in one place. For example, the Ten Commandments found in Exodus 20:2–17 contain many of the features of the early Hittite treaties but not all of them (as the table above illustrates). Various features of the Hittite treaties occur elsewhere in the Pentateuch but not always alongside the account of the drawing up of the Sinai covenant. This brings into question Mendenhall's basic thesis, that the Sinai covenant was modelled from an early stage on Hittite treaties. If the Sinai covenant had been modelled on a Hittite treaty from an early date, one would expect to find all its parts in one place in the biblical account.

Festivals and the exodus

Another question of historicity concerns the establishment of certain cultic regulations: two festivals and the practice of the dedication of the first-born to YHWH. The festivals of the Passover and unleavened bread are associated with the account of the exodus. Exodus 12:1–13, 21–27 and 43–50 sets out the regulations which must be observed at the feast of the Passover. The Israelites must choose a blemish free lamb on the tenth day of the Jewish month of Nisan and keep it until the fourteenth day, when it should be slaughtered. That evening, its blood should be sprinkled on the doorposts of the house and it should be roasted and eaten. Interwoven with this account in Exodus 12:14–20 and 13:3–10 are the regulations for the feast of unleavened bread, which the biblical account states is a seven-day continuation of the feast of the Passover (that is, it runs from the fifteenth to the twenty-first day of Nisan). The festival is marked by the eating of unleavened bread. Exodus 13:1, 11–16 contains the regulations for dedicating the first-born to YHWH.

These three practices, the festivals of the Passover and unleavened bread and the dedication of the first-born, are interwoven with the account of exodus. However, the likelihood of them being performed in this way at the time of the exodus seems slim. Indeed, although the narrative links them closely together, scholars such as W. Johnstone (1990, pp. 39–47) argue that these festivals were originally independent and only later associated with each other within the framework of the biblical narrative. The motivation behind this suggestion is that it seems unlikely that the Israelites, fleeing from the Egyptians, would have had time to observe all the regulations associated with the festivals. In addition, the regulations governing the first-born seems a more general stipulation for action every time a male, human or animal, is born rather than a specific command associated with the event of the exodus. It seems more likely that these cultic regulations were not instituted at the time of the exodus but gained additional significance as a result of their association with the account.

Johnstone, following L. Rost and other scholars, goes so far as to suggest that the festivals of the Passover and unleavened bread originated in different cultures. He associates the Passover with nomadic practices and the feast of unleavened bread with settled, agricultural festivals. He notes the similarities between the Passover and the practice of the Sinai Bedouin tribes called the *fidyah*. This practice was designed to ward off cholera and consisted of smearing the entrance of a dwelling with the blood of a slaughtered animal and consuming its flesh in a community meal (p. 41). In contrast, Johnstone suggests that the feast of unleavened bread originated in a farming community and originally marked the beginning of the barley harvest, drawing his evidence from Exodus 23:14–19 and 34:18–26 which contain additional regulations for the festival.

Whether or not this theory is correct, there can be little doubt that the cultic regulations contained in Exodus 12–13 gained enormous significance due to their association with God's act of redemption in the exodus. Both in Judaism and Christianity these two feasts, together with the associated practice of the dedication of every first-born male, gained central importance. The feast of the Passover and unleavened bread became one of the three obligatory pilgrimage festivals, alongside the feast of weeks and the feast of Tabernacles (see, for example, Exod 23:14–19), celebrated in the temple every year. Consequently it stood at the heart of Israelite worship year by year. Even after the fall of the temple in 70 CE, the festival maintained its importance. *Mishnah Pesahim*, a tractate of the Mishnah, contains regulations for the celebration of the Passover after the fall of the temple. Their reinterpretation of the festival makes it a family celebration, associated with redemption, both past and future. Indeed, this dimension of the Passover festival continues to the present day, with the toast 'next year in Jerusalem' looking forward to a time of future redemption.

The Passover became equally important within Christianity, through its association with the crucifixion and resurrection of Jesus Christ. For Christians, the notion of the dedication of the first-born male, associated with the Passover in Exodus, gives the tradition additional significance. Thus the twin notions of Jesus as the paschal lamb and the first-born son of God are intertwined. The gospel accounts do not agree about the precise correlation between the events of the crucifixion and the feast of the Passover. The Synoptic Gospels maintain that the last supper was the Passover meal celebrated by Jesus and his disciples (Mark 14:6, 12–17; Matt 26:17, 19–20; Luke 22:7–9, 13–14), making the crucifixion take place at the beginning of the feast of unleavened bread. By contrast, John's Gospel has Jesus crucified at the same time as the paschal lambs, on the last day of the feast of the Passover (John 19:14). Either way, the association of the Passover with the concept of redemption makes it an even more appropriate backdrop for the celebration of the Christian notion of redemption.

Exodus in biblical tradition

Just as the festival of the Passover is important in later biblical and extra-biblical tradition, so also the account of the exodus is a central theme in later biblical narratives. The account is used as a model for future events as well as a basis for subsequent theological reflection. The event of exodus became a pattern for other events in Jewish and Christian history, particularly those that involved leaving or returning to a land. The account of entry into the Promised Land across the river Jordan (Josh 4) seems to be consciously based on the crossing of the Red Sea. Likewise the glorious return from exile, envisioned by the prophets Isaiah and Ezekiel, also seems to be based upon the exodus narrative (see particularly Isa 43:14–21; Ezek 20:32–44). Even in the New Testament, God's redemptive act in the incarnation is, on occasion, interpreted in terms of the exodus. Thus the flight of Joseph, Mary and Jesus to Egypt and their subsequent return is interpreted as a second exodus by the author of the Gospel of Matthew (Matt 2:15).

One of the major ways in which the tradition is used in theological reflection is to define and celebrate the salvific nature of God's relationship with the Israelites. It is in the exodus event that God's nature, as one who saves God's people from slavery and oppression, is defined. G. von Rad, in his *Old Testament Theology* ([1957] 1975), defined the nature of Hebrew Bible theology as a 'history of salvation'. If this is accepted, the exodus event becomes one of the central acts in the Hebrew Bible, as it provides certainty not only of past salvation but also of salvation in the present and future for the people of God. There are many interesting examples of the use of the exodus tradition within the Hebrew Bible, particularly in the Psalter and the writings of the prophets (see for example Hos 11:1; Ps 78:12ff.). Especially striking are those psalms which allude both to the exodus and to events in primeval history. Indeed, at times, the psalmists seem to associate the crossing of the Red Sea with either creation or the flood. Interesting examples of this can be found in Psalms 74 and 77. Here references to dividing the sea by might (74:13) seem equally applicable to the act of God's taming of the waters at creation and to the crossing of the Red Sea. In the same way Psalm 77:16–20 seems to blur the crossing with the flood. The biblical writers seem to associate the actions of God in the exodus, creation and flood as similar in type, thus firmly tying the exodus to the primeval history and stressing its association as an event in the story of beginnings.

B. S. Childs has been influential in advocating a study of the Hebrew Bible in general, and the book of Exodus in particular, in terms of the whole of the biblical canon (see Childs, 1974). Childs' concern was a canonical approach to scripture, which was not so much interested in how the biblical text reached its current form but in how the final canonical form of the text interrelated with the rest of the canon. Thus, although Childs' commentary on Exodus explores each passage in detail, it also pauses regularly to reflect upon how it can be understood in the light of the whole of 'Holy Scripture'. This involves not only appreciating the ways in which later biblical writers have used traditions, but also acknowledging that the interpretation of later exegetes has affected the way that we read the text.

Exodus and liberation theology

We have already noted the importance of salvation for an under-standing of the exodus event. The specific nature of the salvation described in the exodus account is of liberation from oppression and slavery. It is unsurprising, therefore, that the exodus account has been one of the crucial texts for liberation theologians. For those who currently experience oppression in any form, the portrayal of a God who hears the cry of the oppressed and acts to liberate them is vital. Liberationist readings of the Bible see its central message as one of liberation for the poor and the nature of God as one who is particularly on the side of the poor. Liberationist readings of the Bible became popular in Latin America in the 1960s and arose out of the reflections of those who experienced poverty and oppression. Unlike other methods of biblical interpretation, it began, not in the academy, but among ordinary people who joined together to read the Bible and share their experiences. Consequently, the most genuine and up-to-date liberationist readings of the Bible are unavailable in print. Helpful surveys of the origins of liberation theology and its impact on the academic world can be found in *The Cambridge Companion to Liberation Theology*, edited by C. C. Rowland (1999).

The significance of the exodus for liberation theology is expressed in G. Gutiérrez's seminal work, *A Theology of Liberation* (1974), as 'the suppression of disorder and the creation of a new order' (p. 88). Gutiérrez notes Moses' struggle not only to achieve liberation for the people of Israel but also to persuade them of the extent of their oppression and their need to struggle against it. Thus the account functions not only as an image of what God has done for the people but also as a model of how people should behave in a situation of oppression. This involves becoming aware of the roots of their oppression, struggling against it and looking forward to a future in which they can 'establish a society free from misery and alienation'. The impact of this approach to the exodus story is that the interpretation of the text becomes a dialogue, with similar experiences shedding light on the text and the text, in its turn, shedding light on those experiences.

An even more thorough liberationist approach to the book of Exodus can be found in G. V. Pixley's commentary on the book (1987). Pixley states that the commentary was written with the dual purpose of understanding the text better and harnessing the 'experiences of Christian believers who are struggling for their liberation'. He attempts to interpret Exodus using insights gained from the socio-political contexts in which the book was produced. Pixley believes that each of the historical contexts that influenced the book left its mark on its pages. He identifies the four major 'moments' or levels in the text as: the actual event; the settlement in Canaan; the founding of the monarchy; and the Jewish life in the Persian Empire (pp. xviii–xx). He maintains that if the text is read from the perspective of these four 'moments' it will help the reader to distinguish the ideologies that lie behind the text.

The figure of Moses

In the section entitled 'Exodus and Sinai' (p. 71), we noted the scholarship of M. Noth ([1954] 1960), who maintained the separateness of various elements of the patriarchal and exodus traditions . His scepticism about the historicity of the account also led him to question the historicity of the figure of Moses, whom he regarded as the editorial glue which joined together the otherwise independent strands (p. 136). More recent scholars such as G. W. Coats (1988) have questioned the accuracy of this view, arguing that the importance of Moses within the tradition indicates that he was something more than an editorial device (pp. 37–8). Indeed, the figure of Moses stands out from the pages of the biblical narrative as much more than a transitional device that joins together various unconnected traditions. Moses is the first leader of the nascent people of Israel, called to be God's agent in one of the most significant acts of divine redemption recorded in the biblical narrative. He is a figure of such importance that it is difficult to imagine the biblical narrative without him.

The Moses birth narratives (1:1–2:25)

The book of Exodus begins with an overview of the 'family of Abraham', now become a great people in a foreign land, but very quickly focuses on one particular member of this people: Moses. The narrative differs from that of Genesis because this is no longer a family history, but it remains similar in that the story is told through the eyes of one person. It consists of a number of vignettes apparently unconnected and many years apart. It begins with the birth of Moses, then moves on to Moses' flight from Egypt in disgrace, his marriage to Zipporah and subsequent calling by God to return to Egypt. In the space of two chapters the history of Moses before his call to confront Pharaoh is told in short, economical yet effective units.

The narrative begins with the account of the birth of Moses in adverse circumstances and recounts how his life is saved by the actions of various women. The Hebrew midwives Shiprah and Puah, Moses' mother and sister and Pharaoh's daughter are all instrumental in saving him from death. The account is enhanced by various twists in the plot: the one who saves Israel is saved from death at birth; Moses' life is threatened by a decree of Pharaoh and saved by Pharaoh's daughter; Moses' mother gives up her son to save him and gets him back as his wet nurse.

The second episode in Moses' life also sees him in danger of death, this time for killing an Egyptian. Here again a certain symmetry enhances the tale: Moses is forced to flee from the land from which he will later deliver the people of God. A similar point is made in by J. Blenkinsopp (1992, pp. 146–7), who observes that the tale of Moses' birth is a familiar one in folktales from many different cultures. He draws attention in particular to the legend of Sargon of Akkad (*ANET*, p. 119), whose mother concealed him at birth in a basket made of rushes and sealed with bitumen. Sargon was later rescued by Akki and raised as his son.

The name given to Moses by Pharaoh's daughter when she saved him has caused considerable debate among scholars. The biblical text ties the name (*mosheh*) to the Hebrew word *mashah*, which means draw. It is unlikely, however, that an Egyptian princess would give a Hebrew name to this baby of unknown origin. Much more likely is that this name originates from the Egyptian *mesu*, meaning son, which can be found in other Egyptian names such as Ahmose and Thutmose (cf. Pixley, 1987, p. 7).

The second major episode takes place in the land of Midian, where Moses defended the daughters of Reuel, a Midianite priest, against shepherds who prevented them drawing water from a well. R. Alter (1981, pp. 56–8) regards this as a 'betrothal type-scene', echoing the stories of both Isaac and Rebekah and Jacob and Rachel. There are certainly close similarities between the accounts, most notably the motif of drawing water from a well. Alter notes, however, that the Moses account seems to be 'so spare a treatment of the convention as to be almost nondescript' (p. 57). Whereas in the other stories the narrative develops the characters of Rebekah and Rachel and their respective fathers, this episode gives only the scantiest details about Zipporah and

Reuel. This mirrors the treatment of Zipporah in the rest of the narrative – she is little more than a shadow in the background of the account. What is interesting about this account is that, just as Moses' flight from Egypt anticipated the exodus to come, so also this narrative contains elements which anticipate future action by Moses. For example, the verb used of Moses' action by the well, *hoshi'a*, comes from the same root as the word *moshi'a* or saviour, Moses' future role in relation to the Israelites. Alter also points out a connection between Moses' action to aid the daughters of Reuel to draw water from the well and Moses himself being drawn from the water of the river (pp. 56–8).

These vignettes at the start of the book of Exodus function not only to introduce the major characters but also to point to what has gone before and what is to come. The betrothal type-scene in Exodus 2:14–22 ties the narrative back into the accounts of the Patriarchs in Genesis. At the same time, motifs such as salvation or drawing water show both the active and passive role of the hero Moses: Moses is both saved and saves; he is drawn from the water and draws water. Although the hero of the narrative, Moses does not stand alone. He is helped, just as he helps others.

The calling of Moses (3:1–7:7)

The next stage of the narrative turns to the events running up to the exodus itself and features the calling and sending of Moses to Egypt. This section appears to contain two parallel accounts of the call of Moses (Exodus 3:1–4:23 and Exodus 6:1–7:7), which source critics have traditionally apportioned to 'JE' and 'P' respectively. These two accounts sandwich an account of failure on the part of Moses and Aaron in persuading Pharaoh to release the Israelites. The first account of Moses' calling contains a theophany or revelation of God. Although the biblical account states that an 'angel of the Lord' appeared to Moses in a 'flame of fire out of a bush', the subsequent account makes it clear that it was God himself that Moses encountered. Theophanies occur frequently in the pages of the Hebrew Bible and this one contains many motifs which occur regularly elsewhere (see, for example, Exod 19; Isa 6; Ezek 1). The theophany takes place on Mount Horeb (elsewhere called Mount Sinai), where numerous other theophanies take place, most notably the great theophany which was accompanied by the giving of the law (see for example, Exod 19). Other motifs which stand out are the presence of fire and Moses' fear in the presence of God. In other theophanies, God's presence is accompanied by similar natural phenomena, such as thunder and lightening or hail, and in most the motif of fear in the presence of God can be found.

One of the most significant episodes of this section is the revelation of the divine name to Moses. In Hebrew the divine name is rendered by four consonants, YHWH, and is consequently known as the tetragrammaton (or four letters). It is well known that the sacredness of the divine name in Jewish tradition meant that it was never pronounced. Consequently the word has no vowels and a pronunciation of the word as 'Yahweh' is a guess on the part of Christian scholars. Within Jewish tradition, whenever the tetragrammaton was encountered, the word *'adonay* or Lord was pronounced instead (hence the rendering in the NRSV of 'The Lord' whenever YHWH appears in the text). In order to remind readers of this fact, the vowels of *'adonay* appear under the consonants YHWH. This is the origin of the form of the name 'Jehovah', which is a combination of the Latin form of the letters of the tetragrammaton with the vowels of *'adonay*. The meaning of the divine name is disputed. Exodus 3:14 associates the name with the verb 'to be', though whether this is an accurate rendering of the form of the word is unclear.

The figure of Aaron appears for the first time in this section alongside Moses. Aaron is an elusive character in the narrative, appearing in 126 verses in the Pentateuch but portrayed varyingly by the authors of the account. He is depicted both as a chosen priest from whom a line of priests emerges and also as a flawed character responsible for inciting the Israelites to create the golden calf. The contrasting ways in which Aaron is depicted by the text has led scholars to explore possible explanations for these differences. Wellhausen (1885, pp. 151–61) argued that this contrast reflected a development in the history of the priestly line. He attributed most of the passages, which presented a favourable picture of Aaron, to the Priestly Writer. As he dates the Priestly Writer to the exilic/post-exilic age, this means that the positive image of Aaron originated at a late stage and the negative image at an earlier stage. This agrees with his basic theory that it is possible to trace three phases in the development of priesthood in early Israel: an initial phase, in which there was no hereditary priesthood; a second phase, in which a Levitical priesthood was dominant; and a final stage, in which the Aaronic priesthood gained pre-eminence. The contrasting portrayals of Aaron, then, reflect an early conflict between the two major priestly houses. A detailed presentation of the theories about the development of priesthood can be found in A. Cody (1969). In this particular section, Aaron is an elusive character who appears for the first time in Exodus 4:14 as a proposed mouthpiece for the nervous Moses. No explanation is given of Moses' continued connection with a brother from whom he was separated both while growing up and while in the Midian desert.

The plagues (7:8–12:32)

Moses' second visit to Pharaoh features the ten plagues which God brought on Egypt to persuade Pharaoh to release the Israelites. They fall easily into three groups of three with the tenth, the death of the first-born son of the Egyptians, as the climax of the narrative, as the table overleaf illustrates. It is this final plague which persuaded Pharaoh to let the Israelites go.

Table 7: The Plagues which afflicted the Egyptians

First set of plagues – connected to the Nile	Second set of plagues – disease brought on by flies	Third set of plagues – plagues from the air
First plague: Pollution of the Nile	*Fourth plague:* Invasion of flies	*Seventh plague:* Hailstorm
Second plague: Invasion of frogs	*Fifth plague:* Disease of livestock	*Eighth plague:* Invasion of locusts
Third plague: Invasion of gnats	*Sixth plague:* Boils	*Ninth plague:* Darkness falling
Tenth Plague: Death of the first-born sons		

Across the Red Sea (12:33–15:31)

The exodus continues with the account of the flight from Egypt (Exod 12:33–39; 13:17–14:31), which is interspersed with the account of the institution of the festival of unleavened bread (Exod 13:3–10) and the command to consecrate the first-born males (Exod 13:11–16). It concludes with Moses' and Miriam's song of triumph after the crossing of the Red Sea and the destruction of the Egyptian force. This song of triumph (Exod 15:1–21) occurs in two forms in the text: a long form in the first person (Exod 15:1–18) and short form in the third person (Exod 15:21). The short form, sung by Miriam and 'all the women', contains the first stanza of the long form sung by Moses. It has long been accepted by scholars that Miriam's song is one of the oldest poems in the Hebrew Bible, later taken up and elaborated in Moses' song, which bears a remarkable similarity to hymns of thanksgiving in the Psalter (see for example, Pss 69 and 101). This theory has proved attractive to feminist scholars who are interested in locating the lost female voice in the biblical text. If this episode can be demonstrated to be both ancient and by a woman, then a strong case can be made for upholding the view that the voice of women has been subsumed by later male biblical writers (see the discussion in A. Bach, 1999). Bach wisely warns of the danger of this approach, noting that the attempt to discover the lost voices of women in the text can often be motivated more by the political concerns of the interpreter rather than by the evidence of historical research (p. 423).

In her 1991 article, L. Eslinger is also interested in the issue of interpretations of the exodus account. She notes the significance of this passage both elsewhere in the biblical narrative and in subsequent Jewish and Christian literature. She contrasts the triumphalism of these subsequent interpretations with the biblical passage itself, maintaining that a 'careful study of Exodus 1–14 reveals no trace of triumphalism or congratulatory comment in the narrator's exposition' (p. 51). Triumphalism is inserted into the text by the Israelites' response to God's action in the songs of Exodus 15. The narrator of the events in Exodus 1–14, she maintains, remains neutral. The purpose of the account is not to present a triumphal image of God but to reveal to both the Israelites and the Egyptians that 'I am Yahweh' (p. 57). Eslinger's approach to the text is interesting in that it attempts to present a 'modern' reading of the text based on principles which oppose those of B. Childs. Childs maintains that it is desirable to read each biblical passage in the light of other biblical passages; Eslinger resists this and reads Exodus 1–14 in its own light.

Concluding remarks

The account of the exodus, found in the first 15 chapters of the book of Exodus, is important both as an independent unit and as part of the overall story of beginnings to be found in the Pentateuch as a whole. On its own, it presents the single most re-interpreted event of the Hebrew Bible, defining many subsequent beliefs about the nature of God and the relationship between God and the Israelites. As a part of the story of beginnings, it represents yet another stage in the beginning of Israel. The close connection between the account of the exodus and the creation of the world points emphatically to the significance of this stage. Just as God brought the whole world out of the chaos of the deep, so also the people of God have been brought out of the chaos of oppression into a new life. The story is not, however, complete. Many more years of wandering in the wilderness are to come before Israel is placed in its garden of Eden, as were Adam and Eve before it.

6

This is the law ...

Transition and consolidation

An examination of the whole flow of the narrative of the Pentateuch reveals that it contains two major beginnings, each followed by a period of wandering and consolidation. Chapters 3 and 4 explored the first of these: the creation followed by Abraham's journey from Mesopotamia to Canaan and the consolidation of his relationship with God through the covenant. Chapter 5 examined the second great beginning, the leading of God's people into freedom from slavery in Egypt. The story of creation recounts the movement from chaos to order; the exodus story recounts a similar movement from the chaos of oppression to the order of freedom. Just as the exodus account mirrors the creation, so also the wilderness wanderings mirror the patriarchal narratives. After the two great periods of beginning come two equally important periods of transition and consolidation. Out of these two periods of transition emerge the two great covenants between God and the people: the first between God and Abraham and the second between God and the Israelites. Chapters 6 and 7 will explore the second of these periods of transition through an examination of the two themes of law and wilderness wanderings. In this second period of transition the process of wandering and covenant formation becomes even more distinct than in the first period, with Abraham. For this reason, these two themes will be explored separately, although they remain closely linked.

The dual themes of law and wilderness wanderings are interwoven in the remaining texts of the Pentateuch. Exodus 16–18 recounts the journey of the Israelites to Mount Sinai, where the narrative pauses for the rest of the book of Exodus, the book of Leviticus and chapters 1–10 of the book of Numbers. This location at Sinai provides the framework for the law codes to be found in Exodus and Leviticus and the preparations for entry into the Promised Land found in Numbers 1–10.

The rest of the book of Numbers (10:11–36:13) recalls the wandering in the wilderness from Sinai to Kadesh to the plains of Moab, but also contains four sets of laws about offerings (Num 15), cleansing (Num 19), land and vows (Num 27–30) and land (33:50–36:13). The book of Deuteronomy is set as a farewell speech by Moses in the plains of Moab and contains a large section of laws, concentrated around Deuteronomy 12–36. This chapter will consider the collections of laws in more detail; Chapter 7 will explore the narrative framework of wilderness wanderings.

There are various different collections of laws to be found in the Pentateuch from Exodus 19 to the end of Deuteronomy. Exodus 20 contains the best-known collection: 'the Ten Commandments', also known as the Decalogue, which is repeated in Deuteronomy 5:6–21. Also to be found in the book of Exodus are the 'Covenant Code' (Exod 20:22–23:19) and a collection of cultic commandments about the setting up of the tabernacle (Exod 25:1–31:17). The 'Covenant Code' or 'Book of the Covenant' takes its name from Exodus 24:7, which recounts how Moses read out the collection of laws to the people of Israel after his descent from Sinai. In addition to these there are the collections of laws to be found in the books of Leviticus and Deuteronomy, as well as the miscellaneous laws in Numbers.

Law, theophany and covenant

Theophany and Mount Sinai

The laws found in the second half of Exodus and the book of Leviticus are presented against the background of a theophany at Mount Sinai (Exod 19:1–25; 20:18–21; 24:1–18; 34:1–10). Like the theophany to Moses described in Exodus 3, the revelation of God prior to the disclosure of the law took place on Mount Sinai/Horeb and involved certain characteristic natural phenomena such as thunder, lightning and cloud. Also present is the motif of fear at the presence of God, which is expressed here in terms of the potential danger that existed for the people who came near the mountain (see, for example, Exod 19:12: 'You shall set limits for the people all around, saying, "Be careful not to go up the mountain or to touch the edge of it"'). The connection between YHWH and Mount Sinai/Horeb is regarded as ancient by many scholars. Numerous religions located the dwelling place of their gods on the top of mountains. Indeed, F. M. Cross (1973) argued that Ugaritic tradition about Baal's residence on the top of a mountain was influential on Israel's belief in YHWH (pp. 147–94). Whether or not this is true, considerable evidence exists which points to a strong, early connection between YHWH and Mount Sinai. Particularly interesting are references in the Psalms to YHWH as the 'Lord of Sinai' (e.g. Ps 68:9), a title which seems to indicate an early belief that Sinai was the dwelling place of God.

Although the essential account of the theophany and giving of the law on Mount Sinai is clear, the details are confusing. For example, the narrative presents a confusing picture of Moses' ascent and descent of the sacred mountain. In Exodus 19:3 Moses ascends the mountain to speak to God, he then descends to speak to the people in 19:7, goes up again in 19:8 and comes down again in 19:14. Exodus 19:20 has Moses ascend the mountain once more and descend again in verse 24. After the communication of the decalogue to the people in Exodus 20:1–17, Moses ascends the mountain once more in 20:21. This confusion has indicated to source critics the presence of numerous sources behind the final version of the text. There is little agreement, however, about how these different sources were woven together to provide the final narrative contained in the book of Exodus. The crucial chapters, Exodus 19 and 24, are particularly problematic. On the whole, however, most scholars are agreed that it is possible to identify the presence of all four sources 'J', 'E', 'D' and 'P' behind the text, though some argue that 'D' and 'P' should be regarded as redactors, not authors.

Covenant and monotheism

It is in the context of this theophany to Moses on Mount Sinai that the covenant relationship between God and the people is defined. Although there are many interlocking and overlapping strands of narrative in this account, the essential structure is clear. The theophany established a two-way relationship between the one God and the people of Israel. The revelation of God established one side of the relationship; the law codes dotted throughout the remainder of the Pentateuch established the other. The formation of this relationship placed obligations on the people which must be fulfilled. Although varied in nature, these law codes create vertical and horizontal structures for Israelite society: the vertical structures stipulate the correct worship of God, while the horizontal ones established obligations between human beings. In various instances, the precise nature of the obligations that exist between humans is dependent upon their relationship with God. So, for example, the laws requiring the fair treatment of slaves, recorded in Deuteronomy 15:12–18, are supported by the Israelites' own experience of slavery in Egypt. Just as YHWH redeemed the Israelites from Egypt, so also the Israelites are obliged to treat their own slaves with fairness and compassion.

One of the significant elements within the covenant relationship, established through theophany and law, was monotheism or at the very least henatheism. The difference between the two is that monotheism requires a belief that only one God exists, whilst henatheism allows for the existence of many gods but requires that only one is worshipped. Absolute monotheism is expressed in only a few places in the Hebrew Bible, the most obvious being Deutero-Isaiah, which makes a monotheistic belief explicit (see, for example, Isa 45:5: 'I am the Lord, and there is no other; besides me there is no god'). Elsewhere, the existence of other gods seems implicit (see, for example, Ps 95:3: 'For the Lord is a great God, and a great King above all gods'), though the command to worship only YHWH remains. The requirements of the covenant relationship, unequivocally expressed at the start of the Decalogue (Exod 20:4–6; Deut 5:8–10), are that YHWH alone is to be worshipped by the Israelites.

Despite this, strong evidence exists throughout the Hebrew Bible that the Israelites regularly failed to fulfil this single most important requirement. In the narrative of Exodus, even while Moses was receiving the law from YHWH, the Israelites formed a golden calf for themselves, which they worshipped as the gods who had brought them up out of the land of Egypt (Exod 32:4). The identity of the calf has been extensively discussed by scholars, with suggestions ranging from the calf being a substitute for the missing Moses, to it being an idol of YHWH, a seat for YHWH, or the representation of another god, either 'El or Baal. A helpful summary of the major theories can be found in J. R. Spencer (1992). Whatever the identity of the calf, the significance of the account is that the Israelites broke the requirements for the correct worship of YHWH right from the start. This attitude continued throughout their history and was repeatedly condemned by the prophets and by the Deuteronomistic historian – so much so, that scholars such as J. A. Sanders (1984) have been driven to say that the Hebrew Bible is not so much monotheistic literature as 'monotheising literature' (p. 50), in the sense that it is constantly seeking to reaffirm monotheism as the central tenet of Israelite belief.

Using the law as an interpretative framework for reading the Pentateuch

On the whole, legal material does not provide interesting reading for anyone other than an expert. The biblical law codes are no exception. Consequently, when they are read, they are read for reference purposes. The major studies of the Pentateuch published in the last century have followed this trend and been more interested in the narrative of the

Pentateuch than in the legal material it contains. In a recent study, however, J. W. Watts (1999) has proposed that the legal material was intended to be read alongside the narrative material of the Pentateuch and that, if the first five books of the Hebrew Bible are read in this way, our understanding of them is improved. Watts notes that the most common references to reading in the Hebrew Bible are to the reading of the law. This occurs both publicly (see, for example, Exod 24:7; Deut 31:11; Josh 8:34–35; 2 Kings 22:10; 2 Chron 34:18; Neh 8:1) and privately (see, for example, Deut 17:19 and Josh 1:8). Furthermore, these references to the public reading of the law refer to the reading of the 'whole law, or at least large portions of it' (p. 22). He concludes that this emphasis on the reading of the law suggests that it was written down with the purpose of reading in mind. From this starting point, Watts explores an interpretation of the Pentateuch which takes into consideration the possibility of a public reading of the Pentateuch and the laws it contains.

Watts demonstrates the existence of other texts from the ancient Near East and Mediterranean which use a combination of stories, lists and sanctions in order to persuade their readers (pp. 36–49). The Pentateuch, he maintains, uses a similar rhetorical strategy to persuade its readers. This view of the Pentateuch transforms the law from being an uninteresting addition to the narrative of the text into a central component of the Pentateuch's rhetorical technique. The interrelation of law and narrative was the element that helped the readers to locate their identity within Israel. The value of Watts' approach is that it allows the title 'Torah' to be used for the first five books of the Hebrew Bible in a way that combines both law and narrative. In Chapter 1 we noted the divergence between the traditional Jewish title for the first five books of the Bible (Torah) and the Christian title for them (Pentateuch). The title 'Torah' has more of a legal resonance and the title 'Pentateuch' has more narrative resonance, reflecting the primary interest of each tradition in these books. Watts' argument allows these two interests to be joined under the title 'Torah'.

Ethics and the law codes of the Pentateuch

The presence of the law codes within the Bible inevitably raises the question of how they should be treated in a modern context. Particularly relevant here is the question of whether they are as binding in the modern world as they were within the Ancient Israelite world. Various different approaches to the question exist and range from an examination of the law codes simply as legal material alongside other ancient Near Eastern legal material, to considerations of the texts which regard them as prescribing behaviour in the modern world. A useful examination of the law codes as legal material can be found in B. Jackson (1984) and an up-to-date presentation of the issues concerning the use of the Hebrew Bible in ethics appears in J. Barton (1998).

The problems of this issue are exacerbated by the fact that the law codes are not complete. They do not contain laws which are pertinent to every question of daily living, even though it is clear from texts elsewhere in the Hebrew Bible that such laws existed. Thus, for example, there is no law contained in the Pentateuch which governs the sale of property, but Jeremiah 32:11 mentions a 'deed of property' which was sealed and which he obtained when he bought the field of Anathoth. This indicates that property law existed in Ancient Israel, even if the law codes do not legislate for it. Jewish and Christian traditions allow for this difficulty in different ways. Jewish tradition supplements the laws contained in the Hebrew Bible with those contained in the Mishnah, a collection of rabbinic laws and sayings compiled around 200 CE. The Mishnah purports to contain oral law given to Moses on Mount Sinai and handed down throughout subsequent generations. Thus many areas which are not legislated for in the Hebrew Bible, are, nevertheless, covered in other Jewish texts. Christian tradition takes the opposite approach and regards many of the laws of the Hebrew Bible as no longer binding upon modern Christians. J. Barton (1998) represents a common Christian approach to the use of the Hebrew Bible in ethics when he says that the purpose of the Hebrew Bible

> is not primarily to give information about morality ... but to provide materials that, when pondered and absorbed into the mind, will suggest the pattern or shape of a way of life lived in the presence of God. (p.128)

An exception to this view of the Hebrew Bible in general and the law codes in particular is the Decalogue. The Ten Commandments have, traditionally, been given a place within Christian ethics denied to the other law codes of the Pentateuch. As early as St Augustine, the Decalogue was used to instruct Christians in morality. They were particularly important for the Reformers and formed the bedrock of much teaching that arose from a Reformed tradition. When used in this way, they were often isolated from their historical and literary context and regarded as a 'primary and permanent' moral code, unlike the other law codes which were considered to be 'derivative' and valid only for their age (W. J. Dumbrell, cited in Watts, 1999, p. 159, n. 86).

Casuistic and apodeictic law

One of the most significant contributions to the study of law in the Hebrew Bible has been the work of A. Alt. In his article, 'The Origins of Israelite Law' ([1934] 1966, pp. 101–71), Alt attempted to uncover how the laws contained within the Pentateuch reached their final form. The variety of material in each of the individual law codes led him to conclude that none of them were composed as a single literary unit but had instead reached their current form through a process of development. Using the technique of form criticism, he attempted to discover the original literary forms of the laws contained in the different law codes. He argued that there are two basic forms of law in the Pentateuch: casuistic and apodeictic. Casuistic laws are expressed with a conditional clause, 'If . . .', and those concerned are spoken of in the third person. An example of this type of law, given by Alt, comes from Exodus 21:18–19:

> If individuals quarrel and one strikes the other with a stone or fist so that the injured party, though not dead, is confined to bed, but recovers and walks around outside with the help of a staff, then the assailant shall be free of liability, except to pay for the loss of time, and to arrange for full recovery.

Apodeictic law, he maintained, exists in a list of short, simple clauses, normally worded in a similar way and expressing a prohibition of some sort. A good example of this kind of law can be found in Leviticus 18:7–17:

> You shall not uncover the nakedness of your father, which is the nakedness of your mother; she is your mother, you shall not uncover her nakedness.
> You shall not uncover the nakedness of your father's wife; it is the nakedness of your father.
> You shall not uncover the nakedness of your sister, your father's daughter or your mother's daughter, whether born at home or born abroad.
> You shall not uncover the nakedness of your son's daughter or of your daughter's daughter, for their nakedness is your own nakedness.

and so on . . .

Another of the features that Alt noted was that casuistic law stipulated for general misdemeanours not necessarily specific to Israel, whereas, on the whole, apodeictic law seemed to contain laws more pertinent to Israel. In addition, Alt found various laws in the Code of Hammurabi that bore the same form as the casuistic laws in the Pentateuch. He therefore concluded that the apodeictic laws of the Pentateuch originated in Israel, probably during the covenant renewal

festival, but the casuistic laws originated outside Israel and were
adopted by the Israelites over time. Although there are no extant
Canaanite laws with which to compare the Pentateuch's casuistic laws,
Alt proposed that the casuistic laws originated in Canaan and were
adopted by the early Israelites after they had settled in the land. Alt's
views have been influential in the field of biblical law and much
subsequent debate about the nature of law in the Hebrew Bible has
been conducted in the light of his argument, though not necessarily in
agreement with it.

The Decalogue

The Ten Commandments exist in two slightly different forms in the
Hebrew Bible in Exodus 20:2–17 and Deuteronomy 5:6–21. The major
differences between the two lists are the motivation behind Sabbath
observance and the prohibition against covetousness. In Exodus 20:11
the reason given for Sabbath rest is following the divine example after
creation; in Deuteronomy 5:15 the reason given is the exodus. Exodus
20:17 records a prohibition against covetousness in which the wife of
one's neighbour is counted among his possessions; Deuteronomy 5:21
contains the same list but separates the wife of a neighbour from the
rest of his 'belongings'. These differences indicate that the Ten
Commandments may have existed in more than one form before they
reached their current form in the biblical text. This observation is made
even more pertinent by the form of the commands contained in the
Decalogue. On the whole, each of the Ten Commandments contains
some form of basic prohibition with, in some cases, additional material.
For example, the third commandment ('You shall not make wrongful
use of the name of the Lord your God, for the Lord will not acquit
anyone who misuses his name', Exod 20:7) contains a basic prohibition
against irreverent use of the name of God, with an additional clause
giving a reason for the command.

Those who seek the original form of the commandments suggest
that they were originally basic prohibitions that have been subsequently
expanded. J. Blenkinsopp (1992, p. 208) suggests that they may have
looked something like the list below:

1. You shall have no other gods before me
2. You shall not make for yourself a graven image
3. You shall not utter YHWH's name for wrong purposes
4. Observe the Sabbath day to keep it holy
5. Honour your father and your mother
6. Do not commit murder

7. Do not commit adultery
8. Do not steal
9. Do not bear false witness against your neighbour
10. Do not covet your neighbour's house.

This list is compiled from the form of the text in the Hebrew Bible. It is possible that the fourth and fifth commandments were not originally positive statements, as they are here, but, like the other commandments, negative prohibitions which have later been made into positive commands.

Even the biblical text itself terms this collection of laws Ten Commandments or Words (e.g. Exod 38:28; Deut 4:13; 10:4). Despite this, however, Jewish and Christian traditions are not agreed on how they should be enumerated or divided. Jewish tradition and the Reformed Churches enumerate the commandments as in the list above, whereas the Roman Catholic Church and the Lutheran Church count commandments two and three in the list above, about false worship, as one commandment and split the tenth commandment, about covetousness, into two. In addition, Jewish tradition splits the list of ten commands into two collections of five; the first positive and the second negative, whereas Christian tradition splits them into uneven groups of three and seven, or four and six, depending on how the list is enumerated.

On the whole, commentators regard the Ten Commandments either as timeless moral instruction or as a historical insight into the workings of early Israelite society. A recent exception to this can be found in an article by D. J. A. Clines (1995), who enquired into the motivations which lie behind the writing and reading of the commandments. In line with the aim of the book as a whole, Clines resisted the natural meaning of the text and asked instead whose interest the commandments served. It is quite clear, from even the most superficial reading of the text, that they are written in the interests of those with property, hence the prohibitions against stealing and covetousness. This approach is supported by traditional historical-critical treatments of the text which question whether these commandments stretch back to Moses, on the grounds that they seem to be written from the point of view of a settled society in which many people lived in houses and owned property.

The Covenant Code

A second collection of laws can also be found in the book of Exodus and is commonly known as the Covenant Code (Exod 20:22–23:19). It receives its name from the reference in Exodus 24:7, which records Moses taking the book of the covenant and reading it to the people.

The code contains a variety of material, beginning and ending with cultic regulations. The cultic regulations at the beginning of the code oppose idol worship and at the end of the code regulate for worship at the three major agricultural festivals of the year, which took place during the barley harvest (the festival of unleavened bread associated with Passover), the wheat harvest (associated with Pentecost) and the fruit and grape harvest (associated with the feast of Tabernacles). Between these cultic regulations are a whole host of general laws that govern the peaceful continuation of society, covering slavery, murder, stealing and other such crimes.

As was the case with the Decalogue, few scholars regard this collection of laws as originating from the time of Moses. References to owning a pit (Exod 21:34) or allowing a vineyard to grow over (Exod 22:5) point to a much more settled time than the period of wandering in the wilderness. However, the lack of any mention of a king has caused certain scholars to date the code to a time after the settlement but before the growth of the monarchy, around the twelfth to eleventh centuries BCE. W. Johnstone, (1990, pp. 53–5) dates the origins of the laws contained in the Covenant Code much earlier than this. He bases his argument on two major points. The first is the similarity that he notes between some of the laws in the Covenant Code and those in the Code of Hammurabi. He cites as an example the famous law of 'an eye for an eye and a tooth for a tooth' (Exod 21:24) which he compares with Hammurabi 196: 'If a citizen has destroyed the eye of one of citizen status they shall destroy his eye' (p. 54). The second major point of Johnstone's argument is the variety of forms that the laws take in the code. He notes four different types of law, thus abandoning Alt's two-fold division (pp. 54–5). This indicates, he maintains, that the laws contained within the code are not a single unit but developed over time as different types of law were assimilated. Thus he argues that the Covenant Code contains laws which were in line with ancient Near Eastern legal tradition but which were subsequently assimilated by the authors of the Hebrew Bible as stipulations within the covenant.

The tabernacle

Regulations governing the correct worship of God can be found both in Exodus 25:1–31:17 and throughout the book of Leviticus. Scholars generally accept that these passages of cultic regulation stem from the Priestly tradition and within source criticism can be attributed to the Priestly Source ('P'). Exodus 25:1–31:17 is primarily concerned with establishing the construction of the tabernacle and the ordination and actions of the priests. Exodus 35–40 repeats much of the substance of chapters 25–31 as it describes in minute detail how the laws contained in the earlier chapters were to be carried out. The tabernacle, the early Israelite tent sanctuary and place of worship, is presented by 'P' as vital within the cultic life of early Israel as it was the central focus of worship, the place where the Ark of the Covenant was deposited and, most importantly of all, the symbol of God's active presence among the people. The tabernacle remained important for Israel's worship until the time of Solomon, when the temple was built in Jerusalem. After this time, the books of 1 and 2 Kings no longer mention the tabernacle, though 1 and 2 Chronicles mention it regularly as located within the temple.

Both in Exodus and elsewhere, source critics attribute the vast majority of references to the tabernacle to 'P'. This caused Wellhausen (1885), among others, to argue that the tabernacle did not exist but was, instead, part of an attempt by 'P' to institutionalize the religion of Israel. This view has not been well supported in the twentieth century, particularly since parallels with the tabernacle have been found in other ancient Near Eastern cultures. The work of F. M. Cross (1981) has been particularly influential in demonstrating that the tabernacle may have existed, though he maintains that it dated to the time of David, not the time of Moses. Although Wellhausen was probably incorrect in assuming that the tabernacle was not historical, he was right to note its importance for 'P'. Within the structure of the narrative, the tabernacle is instituted by the theophany and giving of the law to Moses. It functions, therefore, not only as the place in which the law was deposited but also as the place where God could be revealed. Consequently, the tabernacle symbolized God's dwelling among the Israelites.

Leviticus

The book of Leviticus contains regulations for the maintenance of purity within the nation of Israel, focusing particularly on regulations for worship. The book falls roughly into two sections. Leviticus 1–16 contains regulations governing the actions of priests: chapters 1–10 lay out the requirements for priestly service in the sanctuary, including the correct offering of sacrifices (chapters 1–7), and chapters 11–16 present the laws of purification to be carried out by the priests. Leviticus 17–27 turns to the purity of Israel as a whole and lays out the requirements for holy living by all Israelites. These chapters regulate in detail the day to day life of Israel, laying down stipulations about how Israelites should behave towards one another. Scholars attribute the book of Leviticus as a whole to 'P' but identify within it a 'holiness code' ('H', chapters 17–

26, with chapter 27 acting as an appendix) which may originate from a different period. A discussion of the dating of 'P' and 'H' can be found above in Chapter 2.

Jubilee

Many of the details of the Levitical regulations seem alien to modern society and pertaining only to Ancient Israelite society, although the principles that lie behind the laws are often relevant. A good example of this is the concept of 'jubilee' set out in Leviticus 25, which has been used extensively by the 'Jubilee 2000' campaign for the relief of international debt. The year of jubilee is an important socio-economic concept within the book of Leviticus, although it is unclear whether it was ever practised widely in post-exilic Israel. It was to take place at the end of 'seven times seven years' (Lev 25:8). At the end of each seven-year period, a 'sabbatical year' took place in which the agricultural land lay fallow (Lev 25:17). At the end of seven of these sabbatical years, a jubilee year began, though there is a disagreement among scholars about whether the jubilee year began on the seventh sabbatical year (49 years) or after it (50 years).

The concept of jubilee demands that any land that has been sold due to financial difficulty must be returned in the year of jubilee. This ensures that wealth remains shared equally among families and tribes. Supporters of the 'Jubilee 2000' campaign took up the principle of the return of property to the poor by the rich in a particular year and called upon the governments of first world countries to cancel the debts of the third world countries. This movement was a significant one and achieved a considerable level of success. U. Duchrow (1995) points out, however, that the notion of 'redemption' in Israel was much more radical even than this. In Deuteronomic tradition (Deut 15:1–3) release from debts and pledges took place every sabbatical year, not just in the year of jubilee. The levitical transference of this obligation to the fiftieth (or forty-ninth) year was 'an unequivocal de-radicalising of the laws of Israel and an exacerbation of the position of debt slaves' (p. 172). The principles of fairness and equality are much more far-reaching within Judaism than the release of debts every fifty years.

Leviticus and purity

One of the most influential studies of the purity laws in Leviticus was produced by the anthropologist M. Douglas (1966), in her study of the concepts of pollution and taboo. This study explores the notion of 'uncleanness' from the perspective of comparative anthropology. Her study explores pollution in many different 'primitive religions', including Israelite religion. In the chapter on Leviticus (pp. 42–58), she maintains that 'uncleanness is matter out of place' (p. 41). Thus, in Leviticus the unclean animals are those that do not fit fully into their type. She argues that Leviticus takes up the threefold classification of animals given in the Genesis 1 account of creation: those on the earth, those in the waters and those in the firmament. Each of these types of creature has a prevailing characteristic:

> in the firmament two-legged fowls fly with wings. In the water scaly fish swim with fins. On the earth four legged animals hop, jump or walk. Any class of creatures which is not equipped for the right kind of locomotion in its element is contrary to holiness. (p. 57)

So, for example, animals in the water that do not have fins or scales are unclean (Lev 11:10–12) and so also are four-footed creatures that fly (Lev 11:20–26). The purpose of these regulations, according to Douglas, is to emphasize the completeness of God. Holiness requires the Israelites to imitate the oneness and completeness of God. The avoidance of any 'incomplete' animal is a physical symbol of this desire for holiness. In a later article (1993a), Douglas returned to the question of forbidden animals in Leviticus, noting, this time, how unusual the levitical laws are in comparison with purity regulations in other cultures, where purity regulations function politically to support the *status quo*; in Israel their concern was not so much politics as justice. Keeping the purity regulations served to remind the Israelites of their obligation to maintain justice for all.

Numbers

The book of Numbers, like its neighbour Deuteronomy, is a mixture of law and narrative. However, unlike Deuteronomy, in the book of Numbers law and narrative are interwoven throughout the book, so much so that M. Douglas (1993b) called it a 'law and story sandwich' (p. 101). Laws appear in chapters 5–6; 9; 15; 18–19; 26:1–27:11; 28–30 and 33:50–36:13, alongside census lists and more descriptive narratives. Although the chapters containing law codes in the book of Numbers may appear from their numbering to be haphazard, it is possible to identify three major portions of law in the book, given at Sinai (1–10), Kadesh (15; 18–19) and the plains or steppes of Moab (28–30; 33:50–36:13). Thus, the narrative shapes the giving of the law in the book of Numbers.

The laws contained within Numbers cover a wide range of different topics, governing how the ancient Israelites live together. Of particular interest are four case studies of legal problems. These legal conundrums are represented as problems that arose in the Israelite community and upon which Moses was called to adjudicate. Moses, in his turn, put the case before God, who made a judgement on the matter. Like the other laws in Numbers, these case studies cover a variety of different concerns: the keeping of the Passover by people rendered unclean (9:1–14), the collection of firewood on the Sabbath (15:32–36), the inheritance of property by women (27:1–11) and the inheritance of tribal property (36:1–12). Unlike the other laws in the Pentateuch, these commands are given in response to particular problems, although many scholars believe that they illustrate how laws became established in the ancient world (Wenham, 1997, pp. 42–5).

Deuteronomy

As in the book of Numbers, law and narrative in Deuteronomy appear side by side. Unlike the book of Numbers, however, the law forms a central core (12:1–26:15), preceded (1–11) and succeeded (26:16–34:12) by narrative. The setting of the giving of the law is a speech by Moses to the people of Israel. This gives the book a characteristic hortatory style. Although it flows fairly well from beginning to end, it is not a unified whole. It contains two prologues in the form of an address by Moses (1:1–4:40; 4:44–11:32), a set of curses (27:15–26), a set of blessings and curses (27:11–13; 28:3–6 and 28:16–19) and certain appendices, including the Song of Moses (31:30–32:47) and the blessing of Moses (33:1–29). Despite this, however, there are no grounds for supposing that the book is made up of a collection of entirely separate sources. Instead, most contemporary scholars are agreed that it has reached its current form through a process of expansion, with chapters 4:44–28:68 forming an original core which was later expanded. A fuller discussion of the composition of Deuteronomy can be found in R. E. Clements (1989), pp. 13–22.

Many of the laws contained in Deuteronomy are adaptations of earlier laws found in the Covenant Code in Exodus 20:22–23:19. G. von Rad ([1964] 1966) noted the many similarities between Deuteronomy and the Covenant Code (p. 13) and argued that where differences existed it was clear that Deuteronomy was the later text. Perhaps the most striking illustration of this is a movement away from laws that govern those who live an agricultural lifestyle to those who live in cities. A good example of this is the law of release which, in Exodus 23:10–11, refers simply to allowing land to lie fallow, but is expanded in Deuteronomy 15:1–11 to refer to release from debt. This movement represents a shift towards a more economically sophisticated society.

Alongside the expansion of the Covenant Code lies an expansion of certain cultic regulations. One of the most distinctive cultic themes in Deuteronomy is the centralization of worship in a single sanctuary. The placing of this command in Deuteronomy 12:1–31, at the very start of the section outlining the laws of Israel, emphasizes its importance within the book. Israel should not worship YHWH anywhere but in the central sanctuary. The traditional practice of worship at various shrines throughout the country is condemned. Indeed, it is the importance of the central sanctuary within the reforms of King Josiah, described in 2 Kings 23:1–20, that indicates that the book of the law found by Hilkiah the priest in the temple (2 Kings 22:8) was part of Deuteronomy.

Worship is one of three strands within the commands of Deuteronomy which give the book its characteristic flavour. The other two are the oneness of God and covenant. These three strands are dependent upon each other. Deuteronomy 6:4 begins with the words 'Hear, O Israel: The Lord is our God, the Lord alone' (NRSV), alternatively translated as 'the Lord is one'. This verse is known within Jewish tradition as the *Shema*, from the Hebrew word for 'hear' with which it begins. This one God has formed a special relationship with one people – the people of Israel – through the covenant and calls them to worship him in one place – the central sanctuary.

Concluding remarks

Law is a central element within the Pentateuch and occurs in various forms in four out of its five books: Exodus, Leviticus, Numbers and Deuteronomy. Although different writers present law in different ways, a single theme connects all the law codes of the Pentateuch – the God who has established a special relationship with the people of Israel requires certain actions from them. Within the story of beginnings, law has a special place. It lays down the foundations for the continuing relationship of God with God's people. As such, the laws expand beyond their original context into the rest of Jewish and Christian history and it is the task of each subsequent generation to discover how the requirements laid down by God in the Pentateuch are to be appropriated.

7

He made them wander in the wilderness ...

Wilderness wanderings

The narrative sections in the books of Exodus, Numbers and Deuteronomy describe the journey of the people of Israel from captivity in Egypt to the borders of the land of Canaan. This journey is commonly known as the wilderness wanderings, due to verses such as Numbers 32:13, quoted in the title of this chapter, which give the reason for the lengthy journey through the desert as a punishment from God ('And the Lord's anger was kindled against Israel, and he made them wander in the wilderness for forty years, until all the generation that had done evil in the sight of the Lord had disappeared', Num 32:12). According to these verses, those who left Egypt in the exodus sinned against God by not following his will and, consequently, were punished by not reaching the Promised Land. From that generation, only Joshua and Caleb entered the Promised Land; all the others died before they arrived. This tradition of wilderness wanderings, however, is not present in every text. Other passages present the journey as much more organized, commanded by God and written down stage by stage by Moses. A good example of this also comes from the book of Numbers, where the journey is described as a planned expedition: 'These are the stages by which the Israelites went out of the land of Egypt in military formation under the leadership of Moses and Aaron' (Num 33:1).

Whether the journey was a confused wandering or an intricately planned expedition, its significance remains the same. The journey across the desert allowed the people of God time to prepare themselves as a community for the new beginning that they were to experience. As a stage in the story of beginnings, it was a time of transition and consolidation in which the Israelites could make themselves ready for God's second creation of land – a land in which the people of God could live as a nation.

The route of the wilderness wanderings

One of the major debates about this stage of the narrative concerns the route taken by the Israelites from Egypt to Canaan. The debate focuses on the location of Mount Sinai and how that affects the route taken through the wilderness. These two are unavoidably linked, because the position taken on the location of Sinai affects one's choice of route for the wilderness wanderings. Just as there is difficulty in identifying, with any certainty, the location of the Red (reed) Sea (see above, Chapter 3), so also there exists a problem in locating Mount Sinai. An initial complexity is that the mountain appears to bear two different names in the biblical tradition: Sinai and Horeb. M. Noth uses source criticism to account for this difference and argues that Sinai is used in early texts, whereas Horeb is used in texts from the later Deuteronomic tradition (Noth, [1954] 1960, p. 128).

The difficulty surrounding the mountain's location is not so easily solved. The major problem arises from the vagueness of the biblical text. The way in which the mountain is described could, and indeed has, led to its location being identified anywhere from the southern Sinai Peninsula to modern Saudi Arabia. The first, and traditional, proposal is that Mount Sinai is to be equated with the mountain Jabel Musa, in the southern Sinai Peninsula ((1) on the map opposite). This location seems to be supported by Deuteronomy 1:2 ('By the way of Mount Seir it takes eleven days to reach Kadesh-barnea from Horeb'). Against this location, however, is the lateness of the tradition, which seems to have arisen in the third century CE. A second possibility is that the mountain is to be found in the northern Sinai Peninsula, in the region of Kadesh-barnea ((2) on the map opposite). This location is suggested by the length of time that the Israelites spent in Kadesh ('after you had stayed at Kadesh as many days as you did', Deut 1:46) but seems unlikely, given the description in Deuteronomy 1:2 quoted above. Another theory supporting the northern Sinai Peninsula identifies the mountain with Jebel Sin Bisher, just south of Suez ((3) on the map opposite) and fulfils the criteria of being three days journey from Egypt and eleven days from Kadesh. A fourth suggestion, supported by Noth 1954, pp. 131–2, places Sinai not in the Sinai Peninsula but further east in North West Arabia. The reason for this is the reference to smoke and fire on the mountain, which Noth believes suggests that it was a live volcano. As no active volcanoes exist in the Sinai Peninsula, this pushes the location of the mountain further east to Arabia, where volcanoes are known to have been active around this time.

The route taken in the wilderness wanderings is hard to ascertain.

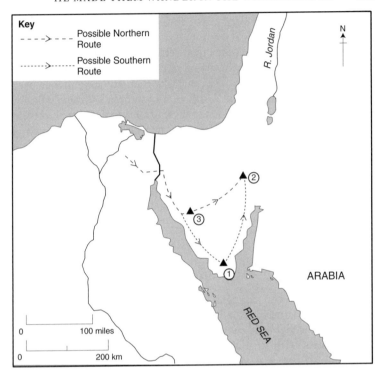

Map 4: Possible locations of Mount Sinai

We know that the Israelites travelled from Rameses to Moab via Kadesh-barnea, but the precise route of their journey is difficult to plot. One factor which affects the route is obviously the location of Mount Sinai. If the mountain is believed to be in the south, then a more southerly route through the wilderness may have been followed; if in the north, a more northerly route becomes possible. A detailed discussion both of the location of Sinai/Horeb and the wilderness wanderings can be found in G. I. Davies (1979).

Exodus

The description of the Israelites' sojourn in the wilderness is concentrated in Exodus 15:22–18:27. The account contains three major sections. The first, 15:22–17:7, describes the Israelites' shortage of water and food in the wilderness and the miraculous provision of sustenance in the form of manna, quails and water. The other two, apparently unconnected, accounts report a battle with the Amalekites and the visit of Jethro, Moses' father-in-law, to the Israelite camp. The account of the visit of Jethro seems to be out of place in the order of the narrative. Exodus 18:5 reports that Jethro visited the camp at the mountain of God, whereas the arrival of the Israelites at this mountain is not described until 19:2. This suggests that the account has been moved out of its natural order. Although out of place chronologically, thematically these three incidents fit together well. They represent three concerns which would have been important for a people such as the ancient Israelites. The three strands of divine intervention to provide food, defence against attack from enemies and the need for internal organisation would have been of prime significance. This short narrative section, therefore, placed as it is between the exodus and the giving of the law on Sinai, presents a cameo of early Israelite life and the factors which were important to them during this period of transition.

Numbers

The book of Numbers contains a much longer description of the time spent in the wilderness by the Israelites. Indeed, the Hebrew title of the book, 'In the wilderness', sums up how important the journey through the wilderness is to it. Numbers is the least distinctive book of the Pentateuch. It begins in the wilderness where Leviticus ends, ends in Moab where Deuteronomy begins, and weaves together material of different types including narrative about the wilderness wanderings, law codes and census lists. It could, therefore, be regarded simply as literary padding for the more important law codes that surround it. Its focus on the theme of wilderness somehow matches its importance in pentateuchal study. The book has a more fluid form than some of its counterparts elsewhere in the Pentateuch. For example, Genesis and Deuteronomy have a much more definitive beginning and ending than the book of Numbers.

For this reason, one of the major questions surrounding the book relates to its composition. Certain scholars such as Noth ([1966] 1968, p. 1) maintain that the book has no unity or structure, whereas others maintain that it has a clear structure which affects the book's message. There is little agreement, however, about the nature of the book's structure. The majority of treatments of Numbers propose a triadic construction for the book, based on the three blocks of material associated with law-giving at Sinai, Kadesh and Moab, though there is little agreement among scholars about where these sections begin and end (see discussion in G. Wenham, 1997, pp. 17–18). A more unusual suggestion on the book's structure has been made by M. Douglas

(1993b). She proposes that Numbers has a cyclical structure which, she maintains, is a commentary on the book of Genesis (p. 98). In her structure the book contains six themes matched by six 'anti-themes'. The six themes describe God's ordering of Israel, the six anti-themes Israel's rebellion against God (p. 101). The difficulty that exists in reaching a scholarly consensus about the structure of Numbers indicates a lot about the nature of the book, which, like the subject it describes, seems to wander from place to place.

One of the greatest difficulties in understanding the book of Numbers is the variety of genres it contains. The book moves, apparently at random, from lists which enumerate the people who followed Moses through the wilderness (chapters 1–4), to purity regulations (chapters 5-6), law codes (15; 19; 27–30; 33:50–36:13), lists of donations (7:12–83) and songs of victory (21:14–15; 21:27–30). In the midst of this miscellany of material is a text, which is frequently quoted:

> The Lord bless you and keep you;
> the Lord make his face to shine upon you, and be gracious to you;
> the Lord lift up his countenance upon you, and give you peace. (Num 6:24–26)

These verses are set between a law which establishes the obligations of Nazirites and a description of gifts brought by Israelite tribal chiefs, with no apparent reason for its position. Indeed, in commenting on this verse, K. Seybold declared that the book of Numbers should be called 'the junk room of the priestly code' (Seybold, 1977, p. 54, cited in Wenham, 1997, p. 40).

The book of Balaam

One of the most memorable episodes in the book of Numbers is the story of Balak and Balaam. Numbers 22–24 contains the account of Balaam, a seer from Pethor in Babylonia who was paid by Balak, the king of Moab, to curse Israel but was prevented from doing so by an angel of YHWH who appeared first to Balaam's donkey and then to the seer himself. The story presents a view of Israel from an outsider's perspective and records the fear felt by the king of Moab at the rise of Israel's power. The account is presented in both prose and poetry and serves to stress the growing importance of Israel even during her time in the wilderness. The best-known element of the story is the account of the talking ass (Num 22:22–35). G. Savran (1994) noted the significance of this account in the light of the only other reference to talking animals in the Hebrew Bible, the serpent in the Garden of Eden

(Gen 3:1–5). Savran noted that an angel with a sword features in both texts (Gen 3:24 and Num 22:31) as do the themes of blessing and curse. When read alongside the Genesis account, further insights can be gained into the story of Balaam and the ass, most notably the progression of theme from universal cursing in Genesis (Gen 3:14–19) to the blessing of Israel by Balaam (Num 23:7-10) – a movement which mirrors the movement of the Pentateuch as a whole.

Deuteronomy

Although most of Deuteronomy consists of law, the book has a narrative framework, in chapters 1–3 and 34, which describe Israel's journey in the wilderness and Moses' death in the steppes of Moab. This narrative serves to give the law a historical context. Noth ([1943] 1981, pp. 12–17) maintained that the feel of a historical survey given by the narrative indicated that it was intended to be an introduction not only for Deuteronomy but also for the whole collection of writings known as the Deuteronomistic histories, which runs from Deuteronomy to the end of 2 Kings. Whether or not this is true, the narrative within Deuteronomy is important because it roots the giving of the law in a particular time and place.

Even more important than the narrative, however, is the fact that the whole of the book is cast as a farewell speech by Moses to the people of Israel prior to their entrance into the Promised Land. This technique of putting speeches in general, and farewell speeches in particular, into the mouths of major figures is characteristic of ancient historians. It can be found not only elsewhere in the Deuteronomistic histories (see, for example, Josh 23) but also in other historical writings in the ancient world. Thucydides, a Greek historian writing in the fifth century BCE, specifically indicated that he placed speeches in the mouths of characters in his histories (*The History of the Peloponnesian War* i.22.1). This technique allows the writers of history to comment on what is taking place. The striking element of Deuteronomy is that the book as a whole is cast as the final speech of Moses before his death. Within the Pentateuch, therefore, it acts partly as a summary and restatement of much of what has gone before. This function of the book is what has given it the name 'Deuteronomy', the Greek for 'second law'. The casting of the book as a speech also gives it a rhetorical flourish and has led scholars such as von Rad ([1964] 1966) to identify its origins in preaching (pp. 15–30).

Concluding remarks

The account of the journey of the people of Israel through the wilderness spans the narrative of three out of the five books of the Pentateuch. The account of the journey is at times, like its content, rambling and drawn out, interspersed with other stories which do not at first appear to fit. This period in the story of beginnings is one of preparation and waiting. The people of Israel are forced to pause in the desert and make themselves ready for the start of their new life in the land that God has promised to them. This is emphasized in the book of Numbers by the forays into the land by spies (Num 13:1–14:39), which turn the attention forward to what will happen, and in the book of Deuteronomy by the restatement of the relationship of the people with God and the consequent behaviour that this relationship demands.

8

Endings and beginnings

We now draw to the close of our story of beginnings. The people of Israel are encamped on the borders of the land of Canaan, ready to enter the land that God has promised to them. This ending is, however, not an ending but a beginning, the beginning of Israel's history as a nation in their Promised Land. The story, therefore, has come full circle from Genesis 1:1. The story began with the creation and the separation of land from watery chaos; it also ends with creation and the separation of the people of Israel from the world around them. The intervening accounts have described the long journey from Eden to Canaan and have followed Abraham and his descendants from their home in the east (Mesopotamia) first to Canaan, then to Egypt, and finally back again through the wilderness to the Promised Land. The Pentateuch ends on the brink of possibility. The future is full of hope. How the people will maintain their relationship with God in this land is the next part of the story.

Reading the Pentateuch

During the course of this book, various different ways of reading the texts have been observed, from those which attempt to uncover how the story reached its current form to those which explore the significance of the text as we now have it. Some approaches to the text attempt to uncover the history that lay behind it; others are more interested in the different themes that it contains. Overall, the impression given is of multiplicity. The Pentateuch contains many different types of material: myth, family or tribal history, laws, genealogies, itineraries and so on. Attempts to interpret the Pentateuch are also many and varied. The task of those who wish to understand Genesis to Deuteronomy better is to pick their way through the many different possible approaches to the text and find those which are most helpful. This book has introduced the text itself and some of the many approaches to the Pentateuch, in the hope that it will provide readers with a guide with which to begin their study of the texts.

Journeying through the Pentateuch

One of the strong images which emerge from the Pentateuch is that of journeying. From the time of Abraham, the narrative follows the travels of God's chosen people, from place to place as they journey towards the future promised to them. In many ways this is a helpful image, not only for the earliest people of God, but also for modern readers of the text. It can be tempting to believe that one should understand the text once and for all and arrive at a final interpretation. The story of the Pentateuch stresses the importance of the lessons that can be learned on the way. Those who read the Pentateuch are also beginning a journey, during which there is much to be learnt.

Further Reading

If you are interested in following up any of the topics touched on in this book, you may like to consult some of the following books. A. J. Hoerth's book on the archaeology of the Old Testament (*Archaeology and the Old Testament*, Grand Rapids: Baker Books, 1997) presents some of the most up-to-date information about recent archaeological discoveries. Unfortunately G. W. Ramsey's book, *The Quest for the Historical Israel: Reconstructing Israel's Early History* (London: SCM Press, 1981), which is the most accessible examination of questions about the historicity of the Old Testament, is now out of print. However, L. Grabbe's book, *Can a 'History of Israel' be Written?* (Sheffield Academic Press, 1997) raises some very important points about the historicity of the Old Testament narratives. People who are interested in discovering more about ancient Near Eastern parallels with the Old Testament will find useful the texts printed in V. H. Matthews and D. C. Benjamin (eds), *Old Testament Parallels* (New York: Paulist Press, 1991).

The impact of Julius Wellhausen's ideas on pentateuchal study has been immense, not least due to his theories about the sources that lie behind it. E. W. Nicholson has recently explored his significance in his book, *The Pentateuch in the Twentieth Century: The Legacy of Julius Wellhausen* (Oxford: Clarendon, 1998). Despite the continuing importance of the Documentary Hypothesis for the study of the Pentateuch, more recent examinations have turned more towards other literary approaches to the books. D. J. A. Clines' study of the Pentateuch was an early example of alternative methods of reading Genesis to Deuteronomy. It has recently been reissued with a section in it reflecting upon the impact of these new approaches to the text (*The Theme of the Pentateuch*, 2nd revised edition, Sheffield Academic Press, 1997). Feminist and liberation readings of the Bible are increasingly popular and there are many different studies available written from these perspectives. A. Bach (ed.), *Women in the Hebrew Bible*, (London: Routledge, 1999) and C. C. Rowland (ed.), *The Cambridge Companion to Liberation Theology* (Cambridge University Press, 1999) both contain articles written by a variety of people and are consequently helpful introductions to different feminist and liberationist readings of the text.

Bibliography

Albright W. F. 1957. *From the Stone Age to Christianity: Monotheism and the Historical Process*. Garden City, NY: Doubleday Anchor Books.

Alexander, P. S. 1990. 'Aqedah.' In *A Dictionary of Biblical Interpretation*, eds R. Coggins and J. L. Houlden, pp. 44–7. London: SCM Press.

Alexander, T. D. 1995. *From Paradise to the Promised Land. An Introduction to the Main Themes of the Pentateuch*. Carlisle: Paternoster Press.

Alt, A. [1929] 1966. 'The God of the Fathers.' In *Essays on Old Testament History and Religion*, ed. A. Alt, pp. 1–100. Oxford: Basil Blackwell. 1966 [1929].

Alt, A. [1934] 1966. 'The origins of Israelite law.' In *Essays on Old Testament History and Religion*, ed. A. Alt, pp. 101–71. Oxford: Basil Blackwell.

Alter, R. 1981. *The Art of Biblical Narrative*. New York: Basic Books.

Anderson, B. W. 1978. *The Living World of the Old Testament*. London: Longman.

Bach, A. 1999. 'With a song in her heart. Listening to scholars listening for Miriam.' In *Women in the Hebrew Bible*, ed. A. Bach, pp. 419–27. London: Routledge.

Barton, J. 1998. 'Approaches to ethics in the Old Testament.' In *Beginning Old Testament Study*, ed. J. Rogerson, pp. 114–31. London: SPCK.

Bechtel, L. M. 'A feminist reading of Genesis 19:1–11.' In *Genesis. A Feminist Companion to the Bible* (Second Series), ed. A. Brenner, pp. 108–28. Sheffield Academic Press.

Bimson J. J. 1978. *Redating the Exodus and Conquest. Journal for the Study of the Old Testament*, Supplement Series 5. Sheffield: JSOT Press.

Blenkinsopp, J. 1992. *The Pentateuch. An Introduction to the First Five Books of the Bible*. London: SCM Press.

Bright, J. 1960. *A History of Israel*. London: SCM Press.

Brueggemann, W. 1982. *Genesis : A Bible Commentary for Teaching and Preaching*. Atlanta, GA: John Knox Press.

Burney, C. F. 1926. 'Christ as the 'ARXH of Creation.' *Journal of Theological Studies*, **27**, 160–77.

Campbell, A. and O'Brien, M. 1993. *Sources of the Pentateuch: Texts, Introductions, Annotations*. Minneapolis: Augsburg.

Charlesworth, J. H. (ed.) 1983. *The Old Testament Pseudepigrapha*. 2 vols. New York: Doubleday.

Childs, B. S. 1974. *Exodus*. London: SCM Press.

Clements, R. E. 1989. *Deuteronomy*. Sheffield Academic Press.

Clines D. J. A. 1990. 'The ancestor in danger: but not the same danger.' In *What does Eve do to Help? and Other Readerly Questions to the Old Testament*, ed. D. J. A. Clines, pp. 67–84. Sheffield Academic Press.

Clines, D. J. A. 1995. 'The Ten Commandments. Reading from left to right.' In *Interested Parties. The Ideology of Writers and Readers of the Hebrew Bible*, ed D. J. A. Clines, pp. 26–45. Sheffield Academic Press.

Clines, D. J. A. 1997. *The Theme of the Pentateuch*. 2nd revised edn, *Journal for the Study of the Old Testament*, Supplement Series 10. Sheffield Academic Press.

Coats, G. W. 1988. 'Moses: Heroic Man, Man of God.' *Journal for the Study of the Old Testament*, Supplement Series 57. Sheffield: JSOT Press.

Cody, A. 1969. *A History of Old Testament Priesthood*. Analecta Biblica 35. Rome: Pontifical Biblical Institute.

Cross, F. M. (ed.) 1973. *Canaanite Myth and Hebrew Epic. Essays in the History of the Religion of Israel*. Cambridge, MA: Harvard University Press.

Cross, F. M. 1981. 'The priestly tabernacle in the light of recent research.' In *Temples and High Places in Biblical Times: Proceedings of the Colloquium in Honor of the Centennial of Hebrew Union College–Jewish Institute of Religion, Jerusalem, 14–16 March 1977*, ed. A. Biran, pp. 70–90. Jerusalem: Nelson Glueck School of Biblical Archaeology of Hebrew Union College–Jewish Institute of Religion.

Davies, G. I. 1979. *The Way of the Wilderness. A Geographical Study of the Wilderness Itineraries in the Old Testament*. Society of Old Testament Studies Monograph Series 5. Cambridge University Press.

Day, J. 1985. *God's Conflict with the Dragon and the Sea*. Cambridge University Press.

Douglas, M. 1966. *Purity and Danger. An Analysis of the Concepts of Pollution and Taboo*. London: Routledge.

Douglas, M. 1993a 'The forbidden animals in Leviticus. *Journal for the Study of the Old Testament*, **59**, 3–23.

Douglas, M. 1993b. *In the Wilderness. The Doctrine of Defilement in the Book of Numbers*. Sheffield Academic Press.

Duchrow, U. 1995. *Alternatives to Global Capitalism. Drawn from Biblical History, Designed for Political Action*. The Hague: International Book with Kairos Europa.

Eslinger, L. 1991. 'Freedom or knowledge? Perspective and purpose in the Exodus narrative.' *Journal for the Study of the Old Testament*, **52**, 43–60.

Exum, C. 1999. 'Who's afraid of the endangered ancestress?' In *Women in the Hebrew Bible*, ed. A. Bach, pp. 141–58. London: Routledge.

Exum, C, and Whedbee, J. W. 1990. 'On humour and the comic in the Hebrew Bible.' In *On Humour and the Comic in the Hebrew Bible. Journal for the Study of the Old Testament*, Supplement Series 92, ed. Y. T. Radday and A. Brenner, pp. 125–41. Sheffield: Almond Press.

Fewell, D. N. 1998. 'Changing the subject: Retelling the story of Hagar the Egyptian.' In *Genesis. A Feminist Companion to the Bible* (Second Series), ed. A. Brenner, pp. 182–94. Sheffield Academic Press.

Fretheim, T. E. 1996. *The Pentateuch.* Nashville: Abingdon.

Goldingay, J. 1998. 'Postmodernizing Eve and Adam (Can I have my apricot as well as eating it?).' In *The World of Genesis. Persons, Places, Perspectives*, ed. P. R. Davies and D. J. A. Clines, pp. 50–9. Sheffield Academic Press.

Gunkel, H. 1895. *Schopfung und Chaos in Urzeit und Endzeit: Eine religionsgeschichtliche Untersuchung uber Gen. 1 und Ap. Joh. 12.* Gottingen: Vandenhoeck und Ruprecht.

Gunkel, H. [1901] 1964. *The Legends of Genesis: The Biblical Saga and History.* 6th edn, New York: Schocken.

Gunn, D. M., and Fewell, D. N. 1993. *Narrative in the Hebrew Bible.* Oxford University Press.

Gutiérrez, G. 1974. *A Theology of Liberation.* London: SCM Press.

Hurwitz, A. 1982. *A Linguistic Study of the Relationship between the Priestly Source and the Book of Ezekiel. A New Approach to an Old Problem.* Paris: Cahiers de la Revue Biblique.

Jackson, B. S. 1984. 'The ceremonial and the judicial: Biblical law as sign and symbol.' *Journal for the Study of the Old Testament*, **30**, 25–50.

Jobling, D. 1986. 'Myth and its limits in Genesis 2:4b–3:24.' In *The Sense of Biblical Narrative. Structural Analysis in the Hebrew Bible*, ed. D. Jobling, pp. 17–43. Sheffield: JSOT Press.

Johnstone, W. 1990. *Exodus.* Sheffield Academic Press.

Knohl, I. 1987. 'The Priestly Torah versus the Holiness School: Sabbath and the festivals.' *Hebrew Union College Annual*, **58**, 65–117.

Kramer, P. S. 1998. The dismissal of Hagar in five art works of the sixteenth and seventeenth centuries.' In *Genesis. A Feminist Companion to the Bible* (Second Series), ed. A. Brenner, pp. 195–216. Sheffield Academic Press.

Laffey, A. 1998. *The Pentateuch. A Liberation-Critical Reading.* Minneapolis: Fortress.

Lambert, W. G. 1965. 'A new look at the Babylonian background of Genesis.' *Journal of Theological Studies*, **16**, 287–300.

Lapsley, J. E. 1998. 'The voice of Rachel. Resistance and polyphony in Genesis 31:14–35.' In *Genesis. A Feminist Companion to the Bible* (Second Series), ed. A. Brenner, 233–48. Sheffield Academic Press.

Lohfink, N. 1994. *Theology of the Pentateuch. Themes of the Priestly Narrative and Deuteronomy.* Edinburgh: T. & T. Clark.

Matthews, V. H., and Benjamin, D. C. 1991. *Old Testament Parallels.* New York: Paulist Press.

McCarthy, D. J. 1963. *Treaty and Covenant: A Study in Form in the Ancient Oriental Documents and in the Old Testament.* Analecta Biblica 21A. Rome: Biblical Institute Press.

Mendenhall, G. E., and Herion, G. A. 1992. 'Covenant.' In *The Anchor Bible Dictionary*, ed. D. Freedman, vol. 1, pp. 1179–202. New York: Doubleday.

Meyers, C. 1988. *Discovering Eve. Ancient Israelite Women in Context.* Oxford University Press.

Milik, J. T., and Black, M. (eds) 1976. *The Books of Enoch. Aramaic Fragments of Cave 4.* Oxford: Clarendon.

Mills, M. E. 1999. *Historical Israel, Biblical Israel: Joshua 2 to Kings.* London: Cassell.

Moberly, R. W. L. 1992. *Genesis 12–50.* Sheffield Academic Press.

Moyise, S. 1998. *An Introduction to Biblical Studies.* London: Cassell.

Nicholson, E. W. 1973. *Exodus and Sinai in History and Tradition, Growing Points in Theology.* Oxford: Blackwell.

Nicholson, E. W. 1998. *The Pentateuch in the Twentieth Century: The Legacy of Julius Wellhausen.* Oxford: Clarendon.

Noth, M. [1943] 1981. *The Deuteronomistic History.* Sheffield Academic Press.

Noth, M. [1948] 1972. *A History of Pentateuchal Traditions.* Englewood Cliffs, NJ: Prentice-Hall.

Noth, M. [1954] 1960. *The History of Israel.* London: A. & C. Black.

Noth, M. [1966] 1968. *Numbers.* London: SCM Press.

Pagolu, A. 1998. *The Religion of the Patriarchs. Journal for the Study of the Old Testament Supplement Series 277.* Sheffield Academic Press.

Pixley, G. V. 1987. *On Exodus: A Liberation Perspective.* Maryknoll, NY: Orbis Books.

Pritchard, J. B. (ed.) 1969. *Ancient Near Eastern Texts Relating to the Old Testament.* 3rd edn. Princeton University Press.

Pury, A. de. 1992. 'Yahwist ('J') Source.' In *The Anchor Bible Dictionary*, ed. D. Freedman, vol. VI, pp. 1013–20. New York: Doubleday.

Rad, G. von. [1938] 1966. 'The form critical problem of the Hexateuch.' In *The Problem of the Hexateuch and Other Essays*, ed. G. von Rad, pp. 1–78. New York: Oliver and Boyd.

Rad, G. von. [1956] 1972. *Genesis.* London: SCM Press.

Rad, G. von. [1957] 1975. *Old Testament Theology.* London: SCM Press.

Rad, G. von. [1964] 1966. *Deuteronomy.* London: SCM Press.

Ramsey, G. W. 1981. *The Quest for the Historical Israel: Reconstructing Israel's Early History.* London: SCM Press.

Rendtorff, R. 1990. *The Problem of the Process of Transmission in the Pentateuch. Journal for the Study of the Old Testament*, Supplement Series 89. Sheffield Academic Press.

Rofé, A. 1999. *Introduction to the Composition of the Pentateuch.* The Biblical Seminar, vol. 58. Sheffield Academic Press.

Rogerson, J. 1974. *Myth in Old Testament Interpretation.* Beiheft zur Zeitschrift fur die alttestamentliche Wissenschaft, 134. Berlin: Walter de Gruyter.

Rogerson, J. 1991. *Genesis 1–11.* Sheffield Academic Press.

Rowland, C. C. (ed.) 1999. *The Cambridge Companion to Liberation Theology.* Cambridge University Press.

Rowley, H. H. 1950. *From Joseph to Joshua : Biblical Traditions in the Light of Archaeology.* The Schweich Lectures of the British Academy, 1948. London: Published for the British Academy by Oxford University Press.

Sanders, J. A. 1984. *Canon and Community.* Philadelphia: Fortress Press.

Sasson, J. M. 1992. 'The Gilgamesh Epic.' In *The Anchor Bible Dictionary*, ed. D. Freedman, vol. II, pp. 1024–27. New York: Doubleday.

Savran, G. 1994. 'Beastly speech: intertextuality, Balaam's ass and the Garden of Eden.' *Journal for the Study of the Old Testament*, **64**, 33–55.

Scholz, S. 1998. 'Through whose eyes? A "right" reading of Genesis 34.' In *Genesis. A Feminist Companion to the Bible* (Second Series), ed. A. Brenner, pp. 150–71. Sheffield Academic Press.

Schüngel-Straumann, H. 1993. 'On the creation of man and woman in Genesis 1–3: the history and reception of the texts reconsidered.' In *A Feminist Companion to Genesis*, ed. A. Brenner, pp. 53–76. Sheffield Academic Press.

Scullion, J. J. 1984. 'Märchen, Sage, Legende. Towards a clarification of some literary terms used by Old Testament scholars.' *Vetus Testamentum*, **34**, 321–36.

Scullion, J. J. 1992. 'The Genesis narrative.' In *The Anchor Bible Dictionary*, ed. D. Freedman, vol. II, pp. 941–56. New York: Doubleday.

Speiser, E. A. 1967. 'The wife-sister motif in the patriarchal narratives.' In *Oriental and Biblical Studies: Collected Writings of E. A. Speiser*, ed. E. A. Speiser, pp. 62–82. Philadelphia: University of Pennsylvania Press.

Spencer, J. R. 1992. 'The golden calf.' In *The Anchor Bible Dictionary*, ed. D. Freedman, vol. II, pp. 1065–9. New York: Doubleday.

Teubal, S. J. 1993. 'Sarah and Hagar: matriarchs and visionaries.' In *A Feminist Companion to Genesis*, ed. A. Brenner, pp. 235–50. Sheffield Academic Press.

Teugels, L. 1994. '"A Strong Woman, who can Find?" A study of characterization in Genesis 24, with some perspectives on the general presentation of Isaac and Rebekah in the Genesis narratives.' *Journal for the Study of the Old Testament*, **63**, 89–104.

Thompson T. L. 1974. *The Historicity of the Patriarchal Narratives: The Quest for the Historical Abraham.* Beihefte zur Zeitschrift fur die alttestamentliche Wissenschaft, 133. Berlin: W. de Gruyter.

Trible, P. 1978. *God and the Rhetoric of Sexuality.* Philadelphia: Fortress Press.

Turner, L. A. 1990. 'Lot as Jekyll and Hyde. A reading of Genesis 18–19.' In *The Bible in Three Dimensions. Essays in Celebration of Forty Years of Biblical Studies in the University of Sheffield*, ed. D. J. A. Clines, S. E. Fowl and S. E. Porter, pp. 85–101. Sheffield Academic Press.

Van Seters, J. 1975. *Abraham in History and Tradition.* New Haven: Yale University Press.

Van Seters, J. 1983. *In Search of History. Historiography in the Ancient World and the Origins of Biblical History.* New Haven: Yale University Press.

Van Seters, J. 1999. *The Pentateuch. A Social-Science Commentary.* Sheffield Academic Press.

Watts, J. W. 1999. *Reading Law. The Rhetorical Shaping of the Pentateuch.* The Biblical Seminar 59. Sheffield Academic Press.

Wellhausen, J. [1883] 1885 *Prolegomena to the History of Israel*. Scholars Press reprints and translations series. Atlanta, GA.: Scholars Press.

Wenham, G. 1987. *Genesis 1–15*. Waco, TX: Word Publishing House.

Wenham, G. 1997. *Numbers*. Sheffield Academic Press.

West, G. 1990. 'Reading "the text" and reading "behind the text". The Cain and Abel story in a context of liberation.' In *The Bible in Three Dimensions. Essays in Celebration of Forty Years of Biblical Studies in the University of Sheffield*, ed. D. J. A. Clines, S. E. Fowl and S. E. Porter, pp. 299–320. Sheffield Academic Press.

Westermann, C. 1988. *Genesis*. Edinburgh: T. & T. Clark.

Whybray, R. N. 1987. 'The Making of the Pentateuch: a Methodological Study.' *Journal for the Study of the Old Testament*, Supplement Series 53. Sheffield: JSOT Press.

Index of Biblical References

31:11; 90
31:23; 10
31:30–32:47; 99
32:1; 75
33:1–29; 99
34:5; 11

Joshua
1:8; 90
4; 78
8:34–35; 90
23; 106
24:2–13; 72

Judges
6:15; 70

1 Samuel
10:19; 70

1 Kings
6:1; 69
9:26; 71

2 Kings
13:23; 3
22:8; 100
22:10; 90
23:1–20; 100

2 Chronicles
34:18; 90

Ezra
7:10; 4
10:3; 4

Nehemiah
8:1–3; 3
8:1; 90
8:3; 4
8:18; 4
9:13; 3
9:17; 3

Job
1:6ff; 37
9:8ff; 32
38:4ff; 26

Psalms
8; 26
68:9; 88
69; 84
74:13–14; 32, 78
77:16–20; 78
78:12ff; 78
86:15; 3
89:10; 32
95:3; 89
101; 84
103:8; 3
145:8; 3
148:5; 3

Isaiah
6; 6
43:14–21; 78
45:5; 89

Jeremiah
2:6; 3
32:11; 91
34:18; 58

Ezekiel
1; 6
20:32–44; 78

Daniel
9:11; 4

Hosea
11:1; 78

Joel
2:13; 3

Jonah
4:2; 3

Malachi
4:4; 4

Ecclesiasticus
1:1–5; 6
24:23; 11
34:8; 6

Matthew
1:1–16; 36
2:15; 78
12:5; 4
23:35; 35
26:17, 19–20; 77

Mark
10:6–7; 3
12:26; 4
13:18; 3
14:6, 12–17; 77

Luke
2:23–24; 4
3:23–38; 36
20:37; 3
22:7–9, 13–14; 77

John
1:1–18; 26
7:23; 4
19:14; 77

Romans
1:19; 3
4:3; 54

Galatians
3; 55
3:10; 4
4:21–5:1; 55
4:22; 3

Colossians
1:15–20; 4

1 Timothy
2:13–14; 33

Hebrews
11:4; 35

1 John
3:12; 35

Jude
14–15; 37

General Index

Lohfink, N.   20–1, 34, 73;
Lot   46, 55, **60–61**

ma'aseh bereshit   6
McCarthy, D.J.   75
Matthews, V.H.   30, 41, 110
Mendenhall, G.E.   74–5
merkabah mysticism   6
Merneptah Stele   69
Meyers, C.   34
Milik, J.T.   38
Mills, M.E.   49, 68
Mishnah   5–6, 11, 77, 91
Moberly, R.W.L.   61
Moses   1–5, 10–11, 30, 42–3, 49–50,
    53, 67–8, 71, 72, 79, **80–5**,
    87–9, 91, 94, 95, 96, 99, 101,
    104, 105, 106
Moyise, S.   19
myth   26
    ancient Near Eastern myths **28–32,
        40–2**
        Adapa, Myth of   30
        Atrahasis Epic   30, 41–2
        Gilgamesh Epic   30, 41–2
        Enuma Elish   31
    definition of 26, 28
Nicholson, E.W.   14, 73–4, 110
Noth, M.   5, 12, 15, 16, 17, 19, 49,
    73, 80, 102, 104

O'Brien, M.   12
oral tradition   15, 19, 48–9, 56

Pagolu, A.   50
Pithom   69
Pixley, G.V.   80
Priestly Source, *see* Documentary
    Hypothesis
Pritchard, J.B.   30, 41, 65, 81
Pury, A. de.   16

Rad, G. von.   15, 16, 25, 45, 49, 61,
    64, 72–4, 78, 99, 106
Rameses   69

Ramsey, G.W.   51, 110
Red Sea   3, 71–2, 78, 84
Rendtorff, R.   19
Rofé, A.   20;
Rogerson, J.   26, 46
Rowland, C.C.   79, 110
Rowley, H.H.   69

Sanders, J.A.   89
Sasson, J.M.   41
Scholz, S.   64
Schüngel-Straumann, H.   33
Scullion, J.J.   30, 48
Sinai, Mount   3, 5, 13, 19, 53, 67,
    71–6, 82, 86, **87–8**, 91, 98,
    102–3, 104
source criticism, *see* Documentary
    Hypothesis
Speiser, E.A.   52
Spencer, J.R.   89
Spinoza, B.   11

tabernacle, the   87, **95–6**
Teubal, S.J.   60
Teugels, L.   63
theophany   63, 82, **88–9**, 96
Thompson, T.L.   51–2
tradition criticism   49, 51
Trible, P.   33–4
Turner, L.A.   60

Van Seters, J.   14, 16, 51

Watts, J.W.   90
Wellhausen, J.   4–5, **11–14**, 16,
    17–18, 42, 51, 58, 70, 72, 83,
    96, 110
Wenham, G.   35, 58, 99, 104, 105
West, G.   35
Westermann, C.   25, 26, 44, 65
Whedbee, J.W.   62
Whybray, N.   19

Yahwist Source, *see* Documentary
    Hypothesis